D0244993

Aiming for Level 4
Writing

Caroline Bentley-Davies

Gareth Calway

Robert Francis

Ian Kirby

Christopher Martin

Keith West

Series editor: Gareth Calway

William Collins' dream of knowledge for all began with the publication of his first book in 1819. A self-educated mill worker, he not only enriched millions of lives, but also founded a flourishing publishing house. Today, staying true to this spirit, Collins books are packed with inspiration, innovation and practical expertise. They place you at the centre of a world of possibility and give you exactly what you need to explore it.

Collins. Freedom to teach.

Published by Collins
An imprint of HarperCollins Publishers
77-85 Fulham Palace Road
Hammersmith
London
W6 8JB

Browse the complete Collins catalogue at
www.collinseducation.com

10 9 8 7 6 5 4 3
ISBN 978 0 00 731359 4

Caroline Bentley-Davies, Gareth Calway, Robert Francis, Ian Kirby, Christopher Martin and Keith West assert their moral rights to be identified as the authors of this work.

British Library Cataloguing in Publication Data.
A Catalogue record for this publication is available from the British Library.

Commissioning Editor: Catherine Martin
Design and typesetting by Jordan Publishing Design
Cover Design by Angela English
Printed and bound by Printing Express, Hong Kong

Acknowledgements

The publishers gratefully acknowledge the permission granted to reproduce the copyright material in this book. While every effort has been made to trace and contact copyright holders, where this has not been possible the publishers will be pleased to make the necessary arrangements at the first opportunity.

p8 *A Hanging* by George Orwell (Copyright © George Orwell, 1931) by permission of Bill Hamilton as the Literary Executor of the estate of the Late Sonia Brownell Orwell and Secker & Warburg Ltd.
p10 *The Big Issue* cover courtesy of The Big Issue.
p12 'In a Station of the Metro' (excerpt of 1 line) By Ezra Pound, from PERSONAE, copyright 1926 by Ezra Pound. Reprinted by permission of New Directions Publishing Corp.
p13 'To the Snake' (excerpt of 9 lines) by Denise Levertov, from COLLECTED EARLIER POEMS 1940–1960, copyright © 1946, 1956, 1958 by Denise Levertov. Reprinted by permission of New Directions Publishing Corp.
p36 'Sonic the Hedgehog crowned most popular video-game character of all time' article courtesy of The Daily Mail 2008.
p38 Interview with Alexandra Burke courtesy of *Mizz* magazine.
p56 *The Thirty-nine Steps* by John Buchan with the permission of A P Watt Ltd on behalf of Jean, Lady Tweedsmuir, The Lord Tweedsmuir and Sally, Lady Tweedsmuir.
p59 Reprinted with the permission of Scribner, a Division of Simon & Schuster, Inc., from A FAREWELL TO ARMS by Ernest Hemingway. Copyright 1929 by Charles Scribner's Sons. Copyright renewed © 1957 by Ernest Hemingway. From *A Farewell to Arms* by Ernest Hemingway, published by Jonathan Cape. Reprinted by the permission of The Random House Group Ltd.
p69 Winston Churchill speech reproduced with permission of Curtis Brown Ltd, London on behalf of The Estate of Winston Churchill. Copyright © Winston S. Churchill.
pp70–1 From *Cirque du Freak* by Darren Shan reproduced with permission of HarperCollins *Publishers* © *Darren Shan, 2000*.
p78 From *Dr Who: The Monsters Inside* by Stephen Cole, published by BBC Books. Reprinted by permission of The Random House Group Ltd.

The publishers would like to thank the following for permission to reproduce pictures in these pages:

Alamy: pp22, 45, 55, 66, 68; Bridgeman Art Library: p24; Corbis: p59; Getty Images: pp6, 26, 34, 35, 54, 62, 63, 69, 77, 86; iStockphoto: pp7, 8, 13, 14, 15, 18, 19, 20, 30, 31, 33, 43, 46, 49, 51, 70, 72, 73; PA Photos: p36; Rex Features: pp9, 47, 56, 71, 78; Ronald Grant Archive: p81; *The Big Issue* p10; *Mizz* magazine p38.

Contents

Chapter 1

AF1 Write imaginative, interesting and thoughtful texts

This chapter is going to show you how to

- Bring your writing to life
- Use real details in your writing
- Choose and plan the right content
- Choose the best words
- Grab the reader's attention.

What's it all about?

It is very important to choose good subjects – and to write about them in a suitable way. This will make your writing interesting to read.

This lesson will
● sharpen the focus of your writing.

Bringing your writing to life means that it has **energy**, **detail** and is **interesting to read**. It should not stop before it has covered your topic in enough detail. But it should not ramble on either.

Getting you thinking

Imagine your team is 2-0 down at half time. The manager gets angry.

> That was poor, lads. Really very poor. You must do better in the second half.

That's not going to work, is it? But what about this?

> You pack of pampered, overpaid, preening primadonnas! That was flipping horrendous! Blind pensioners would get a ball in the box more often than you did. If you haven't turned it around by the time I've got my backside warm in my seat for the second half, I'll have your your jock straps for goalposts.
>
> Who said you strikers could sit down? Get straight back out there *now* and practise what you're paid all that silly money to do. Score goals!

● With a partner, discuss why the second version is likely to make more **impact** on the players.

● Find examples of where the second version
  ● gives more detail (says *what* was bad)
  ● includes powerful description (of the players or how the manager feels).

Glossary

make more impact: have a powerful effect

Now you try it

Now imagine you are the manager of the team. It's the next game and your team are 2-0 down again.

What are you going to say to your team?

First, explain what they did wrong.

Your defending was terrible: you let their centre-forward …

Now create a **striking** and funny insult like the one in the example

	adjective	adjective	noun
You pack of	pampered	overpaid	primadonnas
You bunch of			

Finally, come up with a powerful comparison:

I've seen… move faster than you lot.
Your defence was weaker than…
My baby daughter could… better than that

Development activity APP

The team score in the 53rd and 86th minute and then win the game with a 40 yard net-burster in the last minute of injury time. The manager comes in.

> That was better, lads. I'm pleased.

He needs to sound it! Write out the speech he should have made. Use the opening below if you wish.

> Lads, I'm over the moon…

- Make sure it is lively.
- Make sure it is detailed – but not rambling.
- Make sure you explain what they did well and how you feel.

Check your progress

LEVEL 3	I can write using simple ideas
LEVEL 4	I can write in a lively way making interesting points
LEVEL 5	I can write imaginatively and thoughtfully as someone else

This lesson will
● help you add real-life detail to your writing.

It's much easier to **bring your writing alive** if you're actually picturing – or reliving – something in your mind. Writing is often better if you bring in at least *some* details from real experience.

Getting you thinking

The writer George Orwell worked as a policemen in Burma. One day he saw a hanging.

Here is his account of the experience:

> It was about forty yards to the gallows. I watched the bare brown back of the prisoner marching in front of me. He walked clumsily with his bound arms, but quite steadily, with that bobbing **gait** of the Indian who never straightens his knees. At each step his muscles slid neatly into place, the lock of hair on his scalp danced up and down, his feet printed themselves on the wet gravel. And once, in spite of the men who gripped him by each shoulder, he stepped slightly aside to avoid a puddle on the path.
>
> […] When I saw the prisoner step aside to avoid the puddle, I saw the mystery, the unspeakable wrongness, of cutting a life short when it is in full tide.

● Hear the passage read aloud. Which one detail from the description sticks most in your mind?

Glossary
gait: a way of walking

Now you try it

1 With a partner, find two other details in the passage which help you feel you are really *there* with Orwell.

2 Imagine you have seen a bike being stolen from outside a shop.

With a partner, plan an account of what you saw.

- What did the bike look like? (Think of colours, or small details, like a scratched mud guard.)
- What happened?
- How did the thief move? (Write down some descriptive words.)

Start by thinking of some real details from your own experience.

Development activity

You now have to give a statement to the police.
Write your statement based on the ideas you planned.

1 Make sure you tell them
- who stole the bike
- what the bike looked like
- what the thief looked like
- what he or she was wearing
- did the thief walk off with it calmly or make a dash for it?

2 Use your real details to make your story sound believable.

3 Police are trained to notice and question for details. Show your statement to a different partner. Your partner has to ask questions and decide whether they believe your story. Did your real details help?

Remember

Small details can have a big impact.

Check your progress

LEVEL 3 I can choose some suitable detail

LEVEL 4 I can choose a few powerful details from real-life and from my imagination

LEVEL 5 I can choose vivid detail to bring my text to life

This lesson will
● help you choose and plan the right content.

This means you choose a subject or a type of writing that fits your **purpose** in writing. It doesn't matter how good your writing is if it's doing the wrong job.

Getting you thinking

● Do you think this *Big Issue* seller is likely to sell many magazines?

> *Big Issue.* Get your copy of the *Big Issue*, the magazine that makes you feel guilty for being better off than the homeless.

How does it work?

It's not much of a sales pitch! The seller needs to **plan** it better – and **choose** his or her words more carefully to suit the audience and the purpose.

The seller should start by these questions:

● Who am I trying to sell the magazine to?
● Why will people buy it?
● What's in the magazine this week?

Can you think of any others?

Now you try it

1 In pairs, come up with an answer for each of the questions above, making a list like the one below:

● Mainly shoppers? Mostly middle-aged?
●
●
●

2 Now write a similar plan for a different sales pitch. This time it's for a new pair of designer trainers made from recycled material.

First, make a plan, asking yourself these questions:
- Who is likely to buy the shoes?
- Why will they buy them?
- How much will they cost?

Now try writing a simple sales pitch. Tell your listeners **three** things about the shoes. You could start by saying:

> *Great design but also great for … and…*

Make sure you've covered every bullet in your plan.

Development activity

Santa has let you down. You didn't get your first choice gift, he broke your bedroom window and there were sooty hoof prints all over the carpet. You fire off a complaint.

> *Oi, fatso, yeah, you in the stupid red suit!*
> *Thanks for ruining my Christmas, mate!*
> *Stuff this junk. I don't even like Duffy!*
> *What about my iPod?*

Luckily, it gets stuck in the chimney and you get another chance. Now, **plan** a better response. And **choose** your content carefully.

1 First, in pairs, work out what questions you should ask yourself.

For example:

- What is the job we want done?
- What kind of text will get that job done?
- Who are we writing to?

2 When you have answered these questions, plan the points you want to make and write your letter.

Remember

Always check your text fits your **purpose** and your **audience**.

Plan what you're going to say.

Check your progress

LEVEL 3	I can sometimes choose the right content
LEVEL 4	I can choose and plan the right content for my purpose
LEVEL 5	I can plan, develop and shape the right content for my purpose and audience

Choose the best words

This lesson will
● help you choose the right words.

Choosing the best words means that you **make every word count**. Not just the adjectives and adverbs but the **nouns** and **verbs** too.

Getting you thinking

The poet Ezra Pound describes what it is like to be on a train as it enters a station – when the faces along the platform suddenly loom into view.

> The **apparition** of these faces in the crowd.

One word – a noun – suggests the ghostly suddenness of the faces better than a paragraph of rambling adjectives. *Apparition.*

In pairs, choose which noun best suggests the suddenness of

The ... of the cat through the flap. [slink / clatter / thunderbolt]
The ... of her kiss on his cheek. [brush / plop / thrill]

Can you think of a noun that would work well here?

The ... of the knife in his back.

Now you try it

Read the following description:

> I put a snake round my neck and it hissed. It was very dry. I told everyone it was harmless even though I wasn't sure. It gave me such a buzz! Then I put it back in the grass and stuff and got on with my day. But it left me feeling great all morning.

The poet Denise Levertov describes the experience like this:

> Green Snake, when I hung you round my neck
>   and stroked your cold, pulsing throat
>   as you hissed to me, glinting
>   arrowy gold scales, and I felt
>   the weight of you on my shoulders,
> and the whispering silver of your dryness
>   sounded close at my ears
>
> Green Snake – I swore to my companions that certainly
>   you were harmless!

- Pick out words or phrases that make her description of the snake *snakier* and her sensations more **alive** than the first description.

Development activity

Have a look at this poem:

> I was in the bushes
> Down in the brook.
> An adder came out
> And went over my foot.
> It felt slimy.
> I was really scared.
> I got out a big stick
> And hit it hard.
> It let out a hiss
> And lay dead.
> I was relieved.

Rewrite the poem using more powerful descriptive language.
- Try to choose words that show (a) how the snake moved and (b) how you felt.
- Adders move like lightning so choose words that describe fast reactions.

Remember
Make every word count!

Check your progress

LEVEL 3	I can choose some suitable words
LEVEL 4	I can choose powerful verbs, nouns, adjectives, adverbs
LEVEL 5	I can choose the right word, sentence, paragraph, text

This lesson will
● help you start your work off strongly.

You only get one chance to make a **first impression**. Lose the reader at the start and you may never get him or her back – none of your other strengths will matter then.

Getting you thinking

Murray Wins Tennis Major —— headline

Fiery Scot Powers to First Title —— sub-headline

Andy Murray, the 23-year-old Dunblane dueller, has —— first paragraph – often in bigger print
become the first Brit to win a major championship
since Fred Perry in 1936.

Some people will read no further – they've got all they need. Sports enthusiasts will read on to the finer detail at the end.

● What does the headline tell you here? Why is it needed?

Now you try it

Read these two openings to a short story. Which one does the best job of grabbing your attention?

1

Gregor Samsa is in his early 20s. He lives with his parents and younger sister in Prague. He works as a travelling salesman and finds his job utterly boring. He feels trapped.

2

> Gregor Samsa awoke one morning, from uneasy dreams, to find he had been transformed into a giant cockroach.

- Why? Discuss with your partner what makes your choice exciting.

Development activity

The opening shouldn't be slow or vague. A short sentence, a single word, a snatch of conversation, a quietly stated 'surprise' statement, an intriguing thought, anything that makes us want to know what's coming next: all these will work.

1 In groups, put these five openings in order of 'grab'. Explain your order. How much do you want to read on to find out what's coming next?

> It was the worst moment of my life.

> Once upon a time, far away and long ago, there were three bears.

> "Oi! Four eyes!"

> My name is Lockwood and I am from a pleasant town in the south of England.

> There are eighteen people in this story and here is a list of their names, addresses, and the clothes they are wearing…

2 Write the opening first sentence to the story of the best day of your life. Remember, you're trying to **hook** the reader, so start with something that will make him or her want to read on and find out more.

Start 'in the thick of it'. You can sort out what's going on for your reader later. They'll **want** to know by then.

Remember

Don't give too much detail too soon.

Check your progress

LEVEL 3	I can write a clear opening
LEVEL 4	I can grab the reader's attention with my opening
LEVEL 5	I can start my work vividly, grabbing and holding the reader's attention

Level Booster

LEVEL 3

- I can use some simple ideas
- I can sometimes choose the right content
- I can choose some interesting words
- I can express a simple view

LEVEL 4

- I can bring my writing to life
- I can use real detail in my writing
- I can choose and plan the right content
- I can choose good verbs, nouns, adjectives, adverbs
- I can grab the reader's attention

LEVEL 5

- I can write imaginatively and thoughtfully to interest the reader
- I can plan, develop and shape my writing
- I can choose the right word, sentence, paragraph, text
- I can write vividly and powerfully
- I can develop a convincing viewpoint or voice

Chapter 2

AF2 Produce texts which are appropriate to task, reader and purpose

This chapter is going to show you how to

- Decide what type of writing you are being asked to do
- Write in the correct style for a task
- Use different techniques to interest and entertain the reader
- Develop a viewpoint in your writing.

What's it all about?

Choosing the right form and style for your task, audience and purpose.

This lesson will
● help you to understand different writing tasks.

Every time we write, we need to think about what we are trying to achieve or being asked to do. We then need to think about the type of writing that will help us do this.

Ask yourself why you are writing it. Is it to give someone information, to persuade somebody to do something or to entertain your reader?

Getting you thinking

Imagine you have been asked to complete the following task:

Write a letter to the manager of a holiday company complaining about your recent holiday to Spain.

You are being asked to
● write formally to someone you don't know
● make your disappointment clear
● include details about what was wrong
● make it clear what you want the reader to do.

Here is one student's response to the task:

> My holiday was a nightmare, although it was fab having two weeks off work (always a positive!). The weather was really hot, but the hotel was rubbish! My room was really pants and there was absolutely nothing to do. The sun was shining but we couldn't even use the swimming pool. All of my mates thought it was a really rubbish trip (and the rat incident really finished it off!) This hotel is hopeless and I want my money back now!

● How well do you think the writer has completed the task?

Now you try it

Read the next letter extract and answer the questions below. For each one, find an example from the text to support your answer.

> One of the main problems with the hotel is the quality of the bedrooms. All of the curtains were torn, two of the showers were not in working order and there were dead cockroaches on the balconies and even in the beds!
>
> We were looking forward to making use of the swimming pool as shown in your brochure – imagine our disappointment when we found that it was empty. Given that the temperature was a hot 36 degrees, a cool dip in the pool was something we were really looking forward to. But the most disturbing incident was when our grandmother discovered a rat in the chef's surprise meal…

- Does the writer make it clear why she is writing?
- Does she use formal language?
- Does the writer give specific examples from the holiday?
- Are all the comments relevant to the task?

Development activity

1 Look at the two lists below. In pairs, decide which form of writing or speaking (or range of forms) is best suited to each purpose.

1 Finishing with a boyfriend/girlfriend

2 Reminding yourself to pack your PE kit

3 Arranging to meet a friend who lives abroad

4 Sorting out what time you are meeting your friends at the cinema

5 Apologising to your next-door neighbour for breaking a window with your football

6 Thanking your uncle for a birthday present

7 Asking your favourite celebrity to attend an event at your school

8 Telling all your friends about your football team's recent win

9 Persuading your head teacher to allow a year group disco

A email
B letter
C postcard
D text
E post-it note
F Facebook or Bebo message
G phone call
H talking to them face-to-face

2 Look at this writing task:

> **Write a newspaper article called 'How to help your child when he or she starts secondary school.'**

Think about what you are being asked to do. What kind of text are you being asked to write?

Can you think of five things you would normally find in a newspaper article?

For example,

- a headline
- a picture
- ...
- ...
- ...

Now try to come up with some answers to these questions:

- Who is going to read the article?
- What do you need to tell them?
- How can you make it interesting?

Check your progress

LEVEL 3 | I can usually decide what sort of writing I am being asked to do

LEVEL 4 | I can decide what type of writing I am being asked to do and choose an appropriate form

LEVEL 5 | I can adapt my writing style to the purpose and task.

21

This lesson will
- help you understand how to use the right style for a piece of writing.

When you have decided what type of writing suits your purpose, you need to write in the correct style. Before you begin writing, ask yourself:

- Who am I writing for?
- Is it a formal or informal piece of writing?
- What techniques do writers use when writing this kind of text?
- What kind of language should I use?

Getting you thinking

Imagine you have been asked to complete the following task:

Write the text for a tourist leaflet about your town.
Write a paragraph that will persuade people to visit your area.

You are being asked to

- write a persuasive text
- write formally for people you don't know
- make your writing appeal to a wide range of people of all ages
- describe the attractions in your area.

Now have a look at the following example:

Oundle is a small town in Northamptonshire. It has a lot of Georgian buildings and a really old church. It has a lot of small shops, a market every week and lots of pubs. It has over twenty restaurants, some are quite expensive and others are cheap.

There are quite a few things to do in Oundle. There is a river, a theatre, shops and a cinema. It is a busy town. Oundle is a good place to visit for people of all ages.

- Do you think this would persuade people to visit Oundle?

Now you try it

Now look at the following text. How has this writer tried to make Reading sound attractive?

Fancy a change? Why don't you visit Reading? There's something for everyone to enjoy. Visit the massive range of shops to suit everyone's pocket. Stroll across the newly developed Riverside, choose from over thirty different restaurants from Tex Mex to Italian. Do you enjoy the cinema? There are ten screens in the new multiplex. Or maybe you are more daring and fancy ice skating, dancing in the many clubs, or just relaxing by the riverside. Whatever your age, whatever your interests, there's something for you to enjoy in Reading.

Find examples of how the writer has
- engaged the reader by talking to him or her directly
- chosen good describing words
- started sentences in a variety of ways.

Development activity

Think about the area you live in. How could you describe in it an attractive way to persuade people to visit?

Try and write one paragraph.

Check your progress

LEVEL 3	I can use one or two techniques to persuade people to visit my town
LEVEL 4	I can use different techniques to persuade people to visit my town
LEVEL 5	I can include a good range of different persuasive writing techniques and features

23

This lesson will
- show you how to use different techniques to create suspense.

When we are writing, we need to think about how we can interest and entertain our reader. This is especially true when we are writing stories or poems.

Let's look at some techniques good writers use to do this.

Getting you thinking

Imagine you have been asked to complete the following writing task:

Write a short story suitable for an anthology called *Ghostly Stories and Spooky Happenings*.

You will need to keep readers on the edge of their seats. Have a look at the following examples.

A

It was then, in the corner beyond the foot of the bed, that he heard something shift. His bones were rigid, as cold as iron. He was clamped motionless. Silence. His breath crept into his mouth. Then the sound came again. His eyes were as wide as an owl's and in the starlight he saw the wardrobe door sigh open.

B

I was standing in a stone-flagged passageway. To my left a door stood ajar. Light trickled feebly from beyond it, falling in a wedge across the flags. I saw slug trails and there was a flat, **fungoid** smell. The old woman slipped a hand under my elbow and began steering me along the passageway. Beyond the puddle of light I was virtually blind. Behind me, the old man closed the door.

Glossary

Fungoid: an adjective to describe a musty smell suggesting mushrooms, mould or other fungus.

For each extract, see if you can find
- at least three things that make it interesting
- three phrases that create a scary atmosphere.

Now you try it

1 In pairs, think of some settings for a scary story.

For example,

an old castle
an abandoned school

2 Plan your story by thinking about
- an **opening** (introducing the scene and the mystery)
- how you will develop this in the **middle** (leading to the crisis or most exciting part)
- how you will resolve this at the **end**.

3 Think up some key descriptions.

For example,

a creaking wardrobe
a flickering candle
an old stone statue

Development activity

Now try writing some of the story by starting in the middle. Pick a moment just before something really exciting happens.

You could start by saying:

I looked around the room...
I could see...

Then develop these sentences into a longer paragraph.

Try to write at least three paragraphs.

Check your progress

LEVEL 3	I can understand how using some different techniques makes writing interesting
LEVEL 4	I can use two different techniques to make my ghost story creepy and tense
LEVEL 5	I can include a good range of different techniques to thrill and entertain my reader

25

This lesson will
- help you understand what a viewpoint is
- help you to express a clear viewpoint in your writing.

Some writing tasks ask us to develop a viewpoint. This means we need to show the reader what we think or how we feel about a particular issue.

Getting you thinking

You have been asked to write a speech to the new headteacher of your school, giving your opinion on school uniform.

You are being asked to
- write formally for somebody in authority
- develop your viewpoint clearly
- explain why you hold this view.

Look at the following example.

> Children today are disappointed by the fact they have to wear school uniforms. In modern society we are encouraged to try to become individuals and to develop our own identities and talents. How can this happen if we are all made to wear the same clothing?
>
> When I started secondary school I thought I would have greater freedom and increased independence. I was very wrong. Our first lesson at secondary school did not focus on all the new subjects we would be learning or even the sensible idea of finding our way around the huge new buildings. Instead we were given a huge list of uniform rules . My heart sank and talking to my friends I found out that I was not alone.
>
> The main reason I feel uniforms are a bad idea is that they crush the individual spirit.

- Can you find any words and phrases that clearly tell us what the writer thinks about school uniform?

Now you try it

Have a look at part of another student's speech.

> Schools have a range of reasons for believing that uniform is a necessary fact of school life. Many feel that less well off students will be bullied by their wealthier classmates if they are unable to keep up with the latest fashions. Some also believe that a strict uniform helps enforce discipline and firm control around the school.

This speech makes some good points about the school uniform debate.

But, the speech does not give a clear sense of the writer's own attitude towards school uniform.

Where could the writer have given more clues about his or her own feelings?

- Rewrite the paragraph to develop a clear viewpoint.

Development activity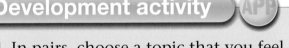

1 In pairs, choose a topic that you feel strongly about, whether it is banning smoking, becoming a vegetarian or paying celebrities less money.

2 Each of you should try to talk about your viewpoint for 30 seconds and then your partner should give the opposite view.

3 Now write three paragraphs explaining your views and making sure that your viewpoint is well developed.

If you like a challenge, try writing from a viewpoint you don't agree with. If you can make this sound convincing, you will have really cracked it!

Check your progress

LEVEL 3 I can sometimes make comments directly to the reader.

LEVEL 4 I can develop a viewpoint in my writing

LEVEL 5 I can use different techniques to develop and signal a clear viewpoint in my writing

Level Booster

LEVEL 3

- I can usually decide what type of writing I am being asked to do
- I can include some of the features of that type of writing
- I can sometimes show I have thought about the reader of my text
- I can discuss whether writing should be formal or informal

LEVEL 4

- I can decide what type of writing I am being asked to do and adapt my writing to the purpose
- I can include the main features of a type of writing
- I can write in the correct style for a task
- I can use different techniques to interest and entertain the reader
- I can develop a clear viewpoint in my writing

LEVEL 5

- I can make the purpose of my writing clear throughout the piece
- I can include a good range of different features for a piece of writing
- I can maintain a viewpoint throughout a piece of writing
- I can adapt what I have read in one form and use the information in a different way in my writing

Chapter 3

AF3 Organise and present whole texts effectively, sequencing and structuring information, ideas and events

This chapter is going to show you how to

- Organise your writing
- Write a clear introduction and conclusion
- Use linking words and phrases
- Make sure your writing stays organised
- Present your work effectively on the page.

What's it all about?

Making your writing easy to follow; setting your writing out clearly and logically.

This lesson will
- show you how to put your writing in order
- show you how to plan your work.

Organising your writing means **putting your ideas into an order** that the reader will be able to follow easily. When we are telling a story or giving someone instructions, it is usually best for our ideas to follow an **organised timeline**. Planning your writing before you start will help you to get this right.

Getting you thinking

If you were writing a recipe for a simple spaghetti Bolognese, you would need to put the instructions in a clear, logical order that someone could follow as they cooked.

- Discuss with a partner how good these instructions are:

You'll need some mince, tomatoes, onion and herbs. Chop up everything, stick it in the pan and cook it for about 30 minutes. Don't forget the spaghetti!

How does it work?

It would be better if the instructions were laid out in a numbered list:

How to make a simple spag bol

Serves four people

Ingredients

1 large onion
300 g of minced lamb or beef
200 g of spaghetti
herbs, salt and pepper

1 tablespoon of oil
1 400 g tin of tomatoes
50 g parmesan cheese

1   Peel and chop the onion.
2   Heat some oil in a large frying pan, then add the onion and cook until golden.
3   Now add the meat and cook on a high heat for 5 minutes until browned all over.
4   Add the tomatoes, season with salt and pepper, and add herbs to taste.
5   Bring the sauce to the boil and then turn the heat right down and allow it to simmer gently for 30 minutes.
6   Serve with spaghetti and some freshly grated cheese.

Now you try it

You are writing some instructions for a friend who is looking after your pet while you are on holiday.

1   Begin by making a plan. Jot down your ideas first and then start to put them into a **logical**, **step-by-step** order.

Remember to think about
- what kind of pet they will be looking after
  (If you do not have a pet use your imagination.)
- what you need to tell them.

2   List the important instructions to ensure your pet is well looked after while you are away.

Development activity

Now write up a clear note to your friend telling him or her exactly what to do, in the order your friend will need to do it in. Add in anything you might have forgotten in your plan.

Check your progress

LEVEL 3	I can put simple instructions in order
LEVEL 4	I can write a set of instructions in a clear, logical order
LEVEL 5	I can write a clear set of instructions using numbering or bullet points

This lesson will
- show you how to write a good introduction
- show you how to write a strong conclusion.

Writing a clear introduction and conclusion is really important, whatever kind of text you are writing. It is especially important when you are making an argument in a speech, an article, or an essay.

A brilliant introduction draws your reader into your subject and **introduces the key point** that you are trying to make.

A clear conclusion shows your reader that you have finished what you have to say. In an argument, the conclusion is often the most important part as it **summarises what has been said**.

Remember

Include a concluding sentence or paragraph in all your written work.

Getting you thinking

Imagine you're taking part in a debate on the topic:

> **Should all teenagers between the ages of 11 and 16 have a curfew of 9.30pm?**

Two opposing **introductions** might be:

> I believe strongly that most teenagers are law-abiding citizens. Why should they be imprisoned in their homes at night?

> Some teenagers cause trouble and terrorise our streets at night. A curfew is a sensible way of stopping them.

Two opposing **conclusions** might be:

> To conclude, I believe a curfew would be unfair to most teenagers.

> Finally, it is clear to me that all teenagers should stay in and do their homework. It would be better for them and for everybody else.

- Can you spot the words each writer has used to show they have reached their conclusion?

How does it work?

Both introductions

- focus on the topic straightaway
- clearly state the opinion of the writer
- are brief and to the point.

Both conclusions

- use words and phrases such as **finally** and **to conclude** to show it is the conclusion
- summarise the writer's argument.

> **Remember**
>
> Use these words and phrases in your conclusion:
>
> In conclusion, / Having taken this into account, / In view of all this, / Finally,
>
> Can you think of any others?

Now you try it

In pairs, you are going to prepare an argument either for or against the motion:

> **All teenagers between the ages of 11 and 16 should have a curfew of 9.30pm.**

One of you will be for, the other against.

1 When preparing your argument, think about
   - how you will open your debate effectively
   - what your main three or four points are going to be
   - what people with the other point of view might say
   - what your conclusion will be.

2 Make a plan before you start. It is a good idea to have six paragraphs:
   - an introduction
   - four main points to discuss
   - a conclusion.

Development activity APP

Once you have prepared your argument, rehearse it and then perform it to rest of the class. The class can decide who had the best conclusion and why.

Check your progress

LEVEL 3	I can write a clear introduction and conclusion
LEVEL 4	I can write a clear introduction and conclusion, which may be linked
LEVEL 5	I can write an effective conclusion which links back to my introduction

This lesson will
- show you what linking words are
- show you how to use them in your writing.

Using linking words helps your writing to flow from one sentence or idea to the next. They allow you to link sentences, to extend ideas and to draw comparisons between them.

Getting you thinking

You can use the following words and phrases to link sentences together in a paragraph:

However
Firstly
Secondly
Clearly
Because
Equally
Most importantly
For example
Finally
On the other hand
In contrast

- Can you think of any other linking words or phrases?
- Can you spot which word or phrase in the example below links the two sentences together?

> I am sick and tired of hearing music blaring from your house late at night. For example, yesterday evening you were playing music by a band called Arctic Monkeys.

Now you try it

1 Write your own pair of sentences using a linking word or phrase **from the list on the opposite page** to connect them.

The first example is done for you:

> The last Amy Winehouse single was excellent. **However**, on hearing her new release this week I couldn't help feeling that she was past her best.

2 Can you explain how the linking word or phrase works in your example? Discuss your example with a partner.

Development activity

1 Your teacher has asked you and a friend to prepare a talk for class tomorrow on a poem you have read. Your friend agrees to come round that night. You will plan it together. But your friend doesn't turn up.

Write a short email to your friend which

- asks why they didn't turn up
- explains how you feel and the problems this will cause
- suggests a way of sorting things out

Use **linking words** between each sentence to link your ideas together.

For example, you could say:

> *Yesterday / Earlier / At school you said that...*
> *However / Unfortunately / Despite what we agreed, you...*
> *This will cause lots of problems. Firstly / Most importantly / Clearly...*
> *So / As a result / Because of this, I think we should...*

Top tips

It is best to use a range of linking words and not the same one all the time.

Check your progress

LEVEL 3	I can recognise and use some linking words
LEVEL 4	I can use linking words and phrases throughout a piece of writing
LEVEL 5	I can use linking words and phrases effectively in all my writing

 35

This lesson will
- show you the importance of keeping your work organised
- show you how to link parts of your work together.

It is really important that your writing is well organised **all the way through** a piece of work. Thinking carefully about the structure will help your reader to follow what you are saying.

Getting you thinking

Read this newspaper article:

Sonic the Hedgehog crowned most popular video-game character of all time.

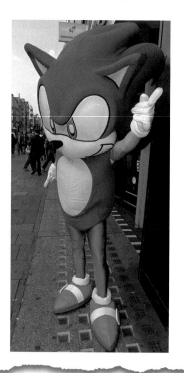

His ultra-distinctive blue spiky look has held the attention of children for years, and now Sonic the Hedgehog has been named the most popular video-game character of all time.

The popular prickly cartoon topped the poll of over 500 gamers, **compiled** to mark the start of the London Games Festival this week.

In a battle worthy of one of his **legendary** games, Sonic held off the challenge of cheeky Italian plumber Super Mario and Tomb Raider's Lara Croft.

Sonic was created by Sega in 1991 and was famous for his special 'spin attack' ability, a skill that saw him roll up into a ball and launch into his enemies.

His debut appearance came on the Sega Mega Drive console and titles starring him are still listed among the biggest sellers on the Nintendo Wii.

The London Games Festival is expected to attract over 100,000 computer games fans to the capital this week.

Daily Mail (23 Oct 2008)

- In pairs, try to work out what point each paragraph is making.
- How does the second paragraph follow on from the first?
- How does the conclusion link back to the opening paragraphs?

Glossary

compiled: put together
legendary: famous

How does it work?

To organise a piece of writing clearly you need to
- make links between your paragraphs
- stay focused on your topic all the way through
- link your conclusion back to your opening.

Now you try it

- Look again at each paragraph. What links can you find between each paragraph and the next?
- Are any particular words or phrases used to link the ideas together?

Development activity

Write a short newspaper article about the best song to play at a party. This can be whatever song you wish – it is entirely up to you.

1 Try to use three or four paragraphs. Plan what you are going to say in each paragraph before you start.

2 When you have finished, go back and check whether your article includes
- ideas that develop from each paragraph to the next
- linking words and phrases that connect one paragraph to the next
- a comment at the end that clearly links back to the start

If not, could you improve your article by using any of these techniques?

3 Re-draft your work, this time making sure you have used all the techniques to improve your writing.

Check your progress

LEVEL 3	I can keep my writing in some sort of recognisable order
LEVEL 4	I can arrange my paragraphs into a logical sequence making some links between them
LEVEL 5	I can clearly signal the direction of my writing by using clear links between paragraphs

This lesson will

- show you how to make your work look attractive on the page
- show you how to present a magazine article.

As well as planning, structuring and keeping your writing organised, it is really important that your work looks good on the page.

Getting you thinking

Have a look at this extract from *Mizz* magazine, which features an interview with Alexandra Burke, the winner of *X Factor 2008*.

Now imagine if the interview was set out with words and sentences and nothing else. It might look something like this:

> Hey Alexandra! Your mum was a singer, is that where you got your love of music? I knew I wanted to sing from the age of five. Mum introduced me to some of the greatest singers – Gladys Knight, Al Green, Whitney, Mariah, Aretha – and whenever she was on tour I'd always be listening to them. And her! Talking of your mum, she gave you a pretty interesting name, didn't she? Alexandra Imelda Cecelia Ewan Burke. See what my mum did to me! I'm named after my mum, my granddad, and my great nan. It's ridiculous. Wow, that's a bit of a mouthful! So what were you doing before you auditioned for The X Factor? I was singing every weekend.

- Discuss with the person next to you which version you would be more likely to read and why.

m celeb

X FACTOR fab!

Another series down and another star in the making, we chat to *X Factor* winner, Alexandra Burke

Alexandra's debut single, *Hallelujah*, is out now!

Hey Alexandra! Your mum was a singer, is that where you got your love of music?
"I knew I wanted to sing from the age of five. Mum introduced me to some of the greatest singers – Gladys Knight, Al Green, Whitney, Mariah, Aretha – and whenever she was on tour I'd always be listening to them. And her!"

Talking of your mum, she gave you a pretty interesting name, didn't she?
"Alexandra Imelda Cecelia Ewan Burke. See what my mum did to me! I'm named after my mum, my grandad, and my great nan. It's ridiculous."

Wow, that's a bit of a mouthful! So what were you doing before you auditioned for *The X Factor*?
"I was singing every weekend

THEY'VE GOT **THE X FACTOR**...
Alexandra joins a whole host of talented winners!

SHAYNE WARD, 2005
Gorgeous Shayne had a No1 hit with *That's My Goal*, as well as three other top 10 singles. He's currently working on his third album – we can't wait!

LEONA LEWIS, 2006
Not only has Leona conquered America and bagged herself a $5 million deal, but her single, *Run*, became the fastest-selling digital release of all time.

LEON JACKSON, 2007
Leon went to No1 with *When You Believe*, and his debut album, *Right Now*, made it to No4.

64 www.mizz.com

Now you try it

Find a magazine of your choice. Look at one page with an article on it.

1 Make a list of exactly what is on the page. Try to include everything you see from the heading to the pictures.

2 How much of the page is taken up by:
- the heading
- pictures
- subheadings
- the writing in the article?

3 What colours have been used on the page? Why?

4 Does the layout of the page make you want to read the article?

Development activity

Work in pairs. Imagine that you work for a magazine. Your editor has asked you to include an article about a famous celebrity (your partner) in the latest issue.

1 Take it in turns to interview each other. The reporter should ask at least three searching questions and the celebrity should give some interesting answers.

2 Now you know your subject, what should you include on the page to make it attractive to the reader?
- Draft out how your page would look.
- Roughly draw in where the headings, pictures and other features would be on the page and put in boxes where you would want the writing to appear.
- What colours would you use? Why?

Level Booster

LEVEL 3

- I can put simple ideas in order
- I can write an opening to a piece
- I can write a concluding sentence at the end of a piece

LEVEL 4

- I can organise my writing into a logical order
- I can write a clear opening and conclusion
- I can use some linking words and phrases
- I can keep my writing organised
- I can present my work effectively on the page

LEVEL 5

- I can structure my work clearly
- I can organise my sentences into proper paragraphs
- I can develop clear links between my paragraphs
- I can develop my material across the whole piece of writing
- I can make my ending link back to my opening

Chapter 4

AF4 Construct paragraphs and use cohesion within and between paragraphs

This chapter is going to show you how to

- Recognise paragraphs and the topic sentence
- Use supporting and ending sentences
- Develop paragraphs
- Arrange paragraphs logically and make links between them
- Use paragraphs when writing letters.

What's it all about?

Using paragraphs organises your writing.

This lesson will
- show you how topic sentences are used.

What is a paragraph? It is a group of sentences about one main idea or subject.

Why do writers use paragraphs? They use them to signal to readers when they are going to write about another idea or subject.

Paragraphs are made up of topic, supporting and ending sentences.

Remember

New paragraphs often signal a change of subject, person, time or place.

Getting you thinking

Look at the five sentences below. They are all about one subject.

> Lord Merganser loved dinner times.
> He loved to slurp his soup with a long silver spoon.
> He loved to feel the soup dribble onto his moustache. He watched with pleasure as it splashed down his new blue shirt.
> He never cleaned up the mess.

- What do you think is the most important sentence?

How does it work?

The most important sentence, or **topic sentence**, is 'Lord Merganser loved dinner times.'

The topic sentence tells us that Lord Merganser loved dinner times. This is the **main subject** of the paragraph. The following sentences then explain why he loved them.

Now you try it

1 Have a look at the following four sentences. See if you can work out which one is the topic sentence.

Sales of big cars are falling. Everyone wants smaller cars nowadays. Small cars cost less. They are also better for the environment.

2 Now have a look at these four sentences. Can you work out which is the topic sentence?

Something strange was going on. Reporters were everywhere. An alien spacecraft had landed. People were scared.

Remember

The topic sentence does not *always* come first.

Development activity

1 Write four sentences about Lord Brockman, who kept and trained white tigers. Use your imagination.

When you have finished your paragraph, underline the topic sentence.

Check your progress	LEVEL 3	I can recognise paragraphs
	LEVEL 4	I can recognise the topic sentence in a paragraph
	LEVEL 5	I can recognise and write using topic sentences

This lesson will
- show you how to recognise other types of sentences in a paragraph.

The other sentences in a paragraph are called supporting sentences and they add detail to the topic sentence.

Getting you thinking

Look again at the first example.

Lord Merganser loved dinner times.
He loved to slurp his soup with a long silver spoon.
He loved to feel the soup dribble onto his
moustache. He watched with pleasure as it
splashed down his new blue shirt.
He never cleaned up the mess.

topic sentence (this introduces the idea or topic)

supporting sentences (these tell us more about the idea or topic)

ending sentence (this completes or closes the idea or topic)

Now you try it

1 Look at the following paragraph. Copy it out and then underline the supporting sentences.

James wanted to be good at football. He dribbled the ball around gateposts and trees. He practised every day. He banged the ball against a wall for hours on end. The players in James' team still thought he was useless.

2 Write a paragraph about somebody who is good at sport. Use a topic sentence, supporting sentences and an ending sentence.

3 Swap books with a partner and highlight the different types of sentences in different colours. You will need three different coloured pens for this activity.

Development activity

1 In pairs, mime a situation where one of you has seen a burglar enter a house and the burglar has seen you. Does the burglar run away? What does the witness do?

If stuck, here is an idea.

- You are eating lunch (mime eating lunch).
- front door on the latch. The burglar creeps into your house.
- The burglar is creeping upstairs. You hear the burglar.
- What happens next?

2 When your performance is over, write down all that happened in the mime. Use a topic sentence, supporting sentences and an ending sentence. (You might need more than one paragraph.)

3 Redraft your paragraph on the computer, using your IT skills.

4 Pass your work to another group. Allow them to suggest improvements. They can underline your topic, supporting and ending sentences using different coloured pens. Did they get it right? If not, talk about it and come to an agreed conclusion.

Remember

In mime, it is your actions that count. No words are spoken!

Check your progress

LEVEL 3	I can write in paragraphs
LEVEL 4	I can write in paragraphs, using a topic sentence and supporting sentences
LEVEL 5	I can write in paragraphs, making clear links between my paragraphs

This lesson will
- show you how to make your paragraphs interesting.

You can develop the main idea in your topic sentence by
- using supporting sentences
- making comparisons
- giving reasons.

Getting you thinking

Look at these examples:

Example 1

> The sea was very rough. Waves lashed against the boat. Some passengers were beginning to feel seasick. Spray splashed onto the deck. The boat lurched from side to side.

The **topic sentence** is 'The sea was very rough.' The following four sentences tell us more about how rough the sea actually was.

Example 2

> The council should not allow the crazy woman to keep hens in her back garden. Allowing hens in a back garden is like granting permission for a zoo to be built on the village green.

This paragraph makes a comparison.

Example 3

> The council should not allow the crazy woman to keep hens in her back garden because other people might want to do the same. Hens are not quiet creatures.

This paragraph gives two reasons why the crazy woman should not keep hens.

How does it work?

It is much better to use supporting sentences than it is to move away from the topic. A bad example would be:

> The sea was rough but the journey only took half an hour. We reached the island by midday. Later we had lunch.

The three sentences above deal with three different topics and each one could be developed into a paragraph.

Now you try it

1 A terrible and destructive forest fire is burning its way to your town.

Start with the topic sentence: 'The forest fire raged.' Now write four more sentences about **how** the forest fire raged.

2 Imagine the fire has reached your town and started to burn down an old factory.

Write three more sentences about the fire – this time **use a comparison**.

3 The fire is burning down the old factory.

Write three more sentences about the fire, **giving reasons** for why it is burning through the factory so easily.

Development activity APP

1 Imagine you are a journalist reporting the fire. You speak to a bystander to find out what he or she saw. Role-play a scene between the journalist and the bystander. How did the bystander feel?

2 The journalist is at home writing in his diary about what has happened. Write the diary entry using paragraphs.

Check your progress

LEVEL 3 I can write diary entries using simple paragraphing

LEVEL 4 I can write interesting diary entries using developed paragraphs

LEVEL 5 I can write interesting diary centries using more complex paragraphing

This lesson will
- help you to order paragraphs logically.

It is important to arrange paragraphs in a logical order and to make links between one paragraph and the next.

Getting you thinking

Look at the story below. It is divided into four paragraphs. However, the story is jumbled up.

Decayed City

a Later, she could see the tramps. They were huddled together. They wore shabby long coats. The tramps rubbed their chapped hands, warming themselves by the open fire. Anna was afraid of them – afraid of what they might do.

b She looked up, to check if the old tenement blocks were about to fall down on her. No crumbling buildings, just the swish, swish of a curtain or two. The oldies were watching her.

c Anna hated walking through Southside. She enjoyed life too much. She didn't want to die. She'd heard about people who'd been crushed to death. Whole buildings had fallen on top of them.

d The oldies never went out at dusk. They were too scared. But they watched everything, everyone. They were watching her now – wondering who she was, what she was doing.

- In pairs, try and work out the most logical order.

Now you try it

1 In pairs, read 'Decayed City' again. What is the topic sentence of each paragraph? What is that paragraph about?

2 How does each paragraph link to the next? See if you can spot any words or ideas that are repeated at the end of one paragraph and the start of the next.

3 The story is not finished. You are going to develop the story by writing two paragraphs of your own. What might happen next?

Think about how Anna might be feeling. Use these thoughts in your paragraphs.

Development activity APP

1 Plan a story, using four paragraphs. Draw a spider diagram first: this will help you to think of ideas.

The story can be about a person who has stumbled into the future.

- How did that person get into the future?
- How is the future different from today? What is better, what is worse?
- How would your concluding paragraph complete the story?

2 You might want to throw a dice – the number that comes up should be the number of sentences in that paragraph.

3 Use your IT skills to write up your story. Then jumble up your four paragraphs. Number the paragraphs. See if your partner can put them in the correct order.

Check your progress

LEVEL 3	I can order paragraphs
LEVEL 4	I can order and write paragraphs, making some links between them
LEVEL 5	I can order and write interesting paragraphs, making clear links between them

This lesson will
- show you how to write letters using paragraphs
- help you to rewrite paragraphs, adding description.

When you write letters, you need to use clear paragraphs. You will need to use all the skills you have learned in the previous pages.

Getting you thinking

Here is a letter from 13-year-old Gemma to her friend.

remember your address

you need the date

this is how to begin

12 Duncane Heights, Colminster CO3 OAL

20th October 2009

Dear Lisa,

We have moved into our new house. We have been here for a whole month! The house is really big and my new bedroom is huge. The wallpaper is gross – it's pink with 'cute' pink elephants doing handstands.

The garden is mostly nettles!

I really miss Halford a lot. I miss the hills and the sea walks. East Anglia is flat! I even miss school but I don't miss old Mrs Perks. She was way too strict. I miss all my old friends, especially you.

I now go to a large comprehensive school. It's called 'The William John Wills School.' Apparently, Wills was an explorer who died in Australia.

My new form teacher is Mr Grigg. He's small and plump and his face wobbles when he talks. The strangest thing is he has a lump under his shirt collar. Sometimes the shirt collar moves. Some people say he keeps a pet bat with him all the time and it stays under his collar. I'm not sure if I believe that!

Dad gave me a new pet. It is a cat. Do you remember Scruffy? He was run over last year. My new cat is black and white. I'm calling him Lucky and I hope he is luckier than Scruffy.

this is Gemma's ending paragraph.

Well, I think I've run out of things to tell you. How is the new term going for you? Please do write and tell me all your news.

Miss you loads, Gemma

- With a partner, can you work out what the topic of each paragraph is?

Now you try it

The letter is very well organised. However, Gemma could have made some paragraphs more interesting by using descriptive words.

Look at the sixth paragraph. It needs some describing words and some extra facts to make it more interesting.

Here is a possible redraft of the first two sentences:

> *Dad has bought me a new pet.*
> *The pet is a lovely surprise.*
> *It's a small fluffy kitten.*

Rewrite the paragraph by adding descriptive words and extra sentences.

Development activity

1 Write a letter to a friend telling the friend all about a strange experience you have had recently. What happened, what did you do?

Use five or six paragraphs and set the letter out like Gemma's.

(If stuck, think about wandering into an old house. You hear noises coming from upstairs. You climb up the creaky staircase and open a bedroom door. There are three children in the empty room. They grin at you. Their faces are white and their eyes glow. Either they are aliens, ghosts or your friends playing a cruel joke on you.)

2 In groups, look at each other's letter. Take a moment from one letter and freeze-frame that moment.

Check your progress

LEVEL 3 I can redraft my paragraphs

LEVEL 4 I can write and set out a letter using paragraphs

LEVEL 5 I can write a detailed descriptive letter using five or six paragraphs

Level Booster

LEVEL 3

- I can write using simple paragraphs
- I can sometimes link ideas between sentences
- I can begin to organise the content of a paragraph
- I can begin to identify the main point in a paragraph

LEVEL 4

- I can identify the main point in a paragraph
- I can recognise how sentences are organised in a paragraph
- I can support my main point with other sentences
- I can link ideas between paragraphs
- I can begin to vary sentences within a paragraph

LEVEL 5

- I can vary the structure of sentences within paragraphs
- I can add pace, variety and emphasis
- I can use paragraphs in a logical order
- I can explore different methods of grouping sentences into paragraphs

Chapter 5

AF5 Vary sentences for clarity, purpose and effect

This chapter is going to show you how to

- Check that simple sentences are correct
- Use simple sentences for effect
- Use compound sentences with conjunctions
- Try out complex sentences

What's it all about?

Using different types of sentences accurately to make your writing exciting to read.

This lesson will
● help you to check that your simple sentences are written accurately.

Every sentence must contain a subject and a verb.

Getting you thinking

1 See how you speak. With a partner, record yourself speaking for 20 seconds about what you did at the weekend.

2 Play back your recording and try to write down exactly what you said.

3 Can you pick out any sentences you have used?

How does it work?

1 A sentence is a group of words that starts with a capital letter and ends with a full stop, question mark or exclamation mark.

2 A sentence can be a statement, a question or a command.

The High Street was busy with shoppers.	(statement)
What's for tea?	(question)
Come in!	(command)

3 A sentence also **makes complete sense**. To do this it must contain two things:

● a **verb** = a **doing** word (*hit* – an action) or a **being** word (*am* – a state)

● a **subject** = a person, place, thing or idea that is doing or being something.

Now you try it

Start with a subject.   Add a 'doing' verb.
    captain   hits

Now add the other words that complete the sense.

    The **captain hits** the ball to the boundary.
         S   V

Now try a 'being' verb.   Think of a subject.   Complete the sentence.
   seems   mother

    My mother seems happier in her new job.
       S   V

- Can you think of one 'doing' verb sentence and one 'being' verb sentence of your own?

Development activity

In *The Pickwick Papers,* Charles Dickens brings in a character called Mr Jingle who speaks in jerky bits of sentences.

Here he is, watching a cricket match with his friends.

> 'You have played it, sir?' inquired Mr Wardle.
>
> 'Played it! Think I have – thousands of times – not here – West Indies – hot work – very. Played a match once – heat intense – couldn't bowl me out – fainted – wouldn't give in – last man left
>
> – sun so hot, bat in blisters, ball scorched brown – five hundred and seventy runs – rather exhausted – bowled me out – had a bath, and went out to dinner.'

If you rewrote the passage in full sentences, Mr Jingle's answer might start like this:

Have I played it? I should think I have, thousands of times. I haven't played it here. I've played it in the West Indies. It was very hot work.

Can you do the same with the last three lines?
- First remove the dashes and commas.
- Then add the words you think are missing.
- Here is your first sentence: *The **sun** was so **hot**. …*

 Check your progress

LEVEL 3	I can write simple sentences
LEVEL 4	I can vary the length and shape of sentences
LEVEL 5	I can build sound sentences of varied lengths and use them effectively

This lesson will

● show you how to use short sentences in a clear or exciting way.

Short simple sentences are perfect for giving clear instructions or writing for younger children.
They can also be used for dramatic effect in stories and poems.

Getting you thinking

In John Buchan's thriller *The Thirty-nine Steps*, his hero Richard Hannay has been sheltering Franklin Scudder, a mysterious stranger, at his London flat. One night he returns home to a shock.

> The lights were not lit, which struck me as odd. I wondered if Scudder had turned in already.
>
> I snapped the switch, but there was nobody there. Then I saw something in the far corner which made me drop my cigar and fall into a cold sweat.
>
> My guest was lying sprawled on his back. There was a long knife through his heart.

● Look at the final two short sentences. Do you think they help to show us the narrator is

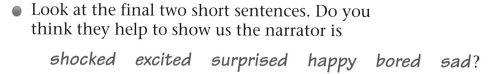

shocked   excited   surprised   happy   bored   sad?

● Do they slow down or speed up the story as you read it?

Now you try it

Write a short, shock sentence to finish off these beginnings. Add an exclamation mark to each!

1 When I got home, I found a parcel lying on the table. I opened it carefully. It was horrible. Inside it…

2 There was a late night knock on my door. I opened it. I could not believe my eyes. It…

3 I turned on the TV news. An amazing thing had happened. The…

Development activity

Short, simple sentences are useful for clarity.

Can you rewrite this set of instructions to be clearer?

See if you can cut it down to five or six short simple sentences that can be read at a glance.

> ### What to do if you hear the fire alarm
>
> When the fire alarm sounds, stop what you're doing, even if it's really interesting or important, and move as quickly as you can to the nearest fire exit, if you know where this is. Whatever you do, don't stop to pick up your belongings like bags or pencil cases or your coat, even if it is cold outside, as fires can burn really quickly and you need to get out fast.
>
> Once you have got outside you should go to your usual assembly point away from the building and check that everyone has made it outside safely.

1 What is the key information? Get rid of everything else.

2 Rewrite the sentence as a command.

The first sentence has been done for you as an example:

~~When the fire alarm sounds,~~ stop what you're doing, ~~even if it's really interesting or important,~~ ~~and~~ move ~~as~~ quickly ~~as you can~~ to the nearest fire exit ~~if you know where this is.~~

- *Stop what you're doing.*
- *Move quickly to the nearest fire exit.*

Check your progress

LEVEL 3	I can use simple sentences
LEVEL 4	I can vary the length and shape of sentences for effect
LEVEL 5	I can use accurate short or long sentences for a purpose

57

This lesson will
- tell you how to use coordinating conjunctions to make compound sentences.

To write really well, you are going to need a variety of sentence patterns including **compound sentences**.

Getting you thinking

You can join two or more simple sentences together to make a compound sentence, using

and   but   or   yet   either/or   neither/nor

1 Here are two simple sentences, each with a subject and verb:

> Suleyman went to the bank. Suleyman withdrew £50.
>   S   V   S   V

Join them together with a conjunction, **and**.
You don't need to repeat the name.

> Suleyman went to the bank **and** withdrew £50.

2 **But** and **yet** suggest a contrast.

> Roisin does her share of the cleaning **but** Carol scarcely bothers.

> I loved her **yet** I did not want to see her.

3 If there is a choice, use **either/or**. For a negative choice, use **neither/nor**.

> I will **either** meet you on Tuesday **or** see you the following week.

> You will **neither** write to him **nor** attempt to see him.

Now you try it

Join these pairs of sentences together with a conjunction.

and but or yet either/or neither/nor

1 Imran took the bus into town. He visited the new shopping centre.

2 Sabine works hard. Lazy Emma got higher marks in the exam.

3 Poland did not do well in the World Cup. Ivory Coast did not do well in the World Cup.

4 You must try harder. You will not succeed.

Development activity

Sometimes simple and compound sentences are perfect for describing fast-moving situations.

> Then there was a flash, and a roar that started white and went red and on and on in a rushing wind. In the jolt of my head I heard somebody crying. I thought somebody was screaming. I tried to move but I could not move. My legs felt warm and wet and my shoes were wet and warm inside. I knew that I was hit and leaned over and put my hand on my knee. My knee wasn't there. My hand went in and my knee was down on my shin. I wiped my hand on my shirt and I looked at my leg and was very afraid.
>
> Ernest Hemingway, *A Farewell to Arms*

1 Which sentence do you find most powerful?

2 Imagine you are walking along a river, when you accidentally slip and fall in. You are desperately trying to stay afloat and reach the bank. You have also injured yourself badly in the fall.

Use a series of simple and compound sentences to describe what is happening.

How gory are your injuries? Give details!

Check your progress

LEVEL 3	I can use some longer sentences
LEVEL 4	I can use conjunctions to build longer sentences
LEVEL 5	I can use simple and compound sentences for effect

4 Try out complex sentences

This lesson will

- explain how to write complex sentences with **if, when** and **because**.

Simple and compound sentences are very useful for clarity, but they can sound repetitive if you use them all the time. To express everything you want to say, you will also need to use complex sentences.

Getting you thinking

You can add information to a simple sentence by using **when**, **if** and **because**.

Look at this simple sentence:

I am tired today.

Could you give some more information about why you are tired?

I am tired today **because** I stayed up late last night.

Can you add some extra information to these sentences to make them more interesting?

It was funny when ...
I can't wait until lunchtime because ...
I can go out this weekend if ...

How does it work?

When, **because** and **if** are **conjunctions** (joining words). They help you to say how, when or why something has happened, or will happen.

You don't always have to add the extra information at the end of the sentence. It can also go at the start or middle of the sentence.

They couldn't stop talking, **when** they finally met.
When they finally met, they couldn't stop talking.
They couldn't, **when** they finally met, stop talking.

Try not to always start your sentences with a **pronoun** (I, you, he, she, they, it) or a **name** (Stella, Priya, Mr Jones). Starting your sentences in different ways will stop your reader getting bored.

Now you try it

You are writing a short email about yourself to your exchange partner from another country. Write four sentences telling your exchange partner about your life, your friends and family, and how you are looking forward to your partner's visit.

Try to write

- one sentence using **because**
- one sentence using **when**
- one sentence using **if**.

Make sure all your sentences don't start with 'I'.

Here are a few ideas to help you.

Because I love sport, I …
When you come and stay, we can…
If you want to get in touch, just …

Development activity

When, **if** and **because** are not the only conjunctions (joining words) you can use. You can also try these words and phrases:

since	unless	although	so	how	until
where	wherever	before	after as	as long as	as soon as
as if	after that	before that	though	while	

See how many of these conjunctions you can use in the next task.

You are writing a list of five top tips for a magazine. You can choose your own topic or pick one from the list below.

How to look good
How to keep a secret
How to tell if he / she fancies you

Your list should give readers advice about the topic you choose. In each tip, try to use one of the words or phrases from the table above.

Check your progress

LEVEL 3 I can try to write some longer sentences

LEVEL 4 I can use conjunctions to build compound sentences and try out complex sentences

LEVEL 5 I can build complex sentences and use them for effect

Level Booster

LEVEL 3

- I can write simple sentences
- I can use some conjunctions and connectives
- I can use capital letters to begin sentences and full stops to end them

LEVEL 4

- I can check that simple sentences are correct
- I can use compound sentences with **and, but** and **or**
- I can try out complex sentences using **when**, **if** and **because**

LEVEL 5

- I can use various kinds of subordinate clause
- I can think about sentence length and structure, and about word order
- I can apply the forms and tenses of verbs

Chapter 6

AF6 Write with technical accuracy of syntax and punctuation in phrases, clauses and sentences

This chapter is going to show you how to

- Use commas in lists
- Punctuate and set out written speech
- Use bracketing commas.

What's it all about?

Using punctuation to make your writing clearer.

This lesson will

● show you how to use commas in lists.

It is easy to go wrong with commas. It is best to only use them when you are sure that they are correct.

Getting you thinking

1 **Commas** replace and or but in a **list of items**. The final and, without a comma, is usually kept before the last item.

> In her schoolbag Kasia kept exercise books, textbooks, pens, pencils, a calculator and her mobile phone.

2 Commas also divide a **list of adjectives** used to describe a person, place, thing or idea. Here is a list by Charles Dickens describing the miser Scrooge in *A Christmas Carol*:

> Scrooge! a squeezing, wrenching, grasping, scraping, clutching, **covetous** old sinner!

3 You can also divide a **list of verbs** (Scrooge again!):

> The cold within him froze his old features, nipped his pointed nose, shrivelled his cheek, stiffened his **gait**.

Glossary

gait: a way of walking.

covetous: jealous of other people's things

4 Here is Dickens again, this time describing a train journey of the 1840s in his novel, *Dombey and Son*. Here the commas divide a **list of phrases**.

> Away, with a shriek, and a roar, and a rattle, through the fields, through the woods, through the corn, through the hay, by the heath, by the orchard, by the park, by the garden, over the canal, across the river, where the sheep are feeding, where the barge is floating, where the dead are lying, where the factory is smoking, where the stream is running, where the great cathedral rises, away, with a shriek, and a roar, and a rattle.

● In pairs, read the sentence aloud, pausing for breath at each comma. What does the rhythm of this long sentence remind you of?

Now you try it

1 Write some list sentences of your own. First, try one with nouns.

> My *best friends are...* (add the list)
> My *dream football team would include...* (add the names)

2 Now try a list of adjectives.

> A _____ _____ _____ *woman entered the room.*

3 Finally, try a list of verbs.

> *To show her fitness, Taleyah...* (swam, jumped, ran, rode)

Add a word or two to each verb to make it livelier: 'swam ten lengths', for example.

4 Read the extract from *Dombey and Son* again.

Write your own description of a car journey **or** a bus ride **or** a cycle ride in the same style, writing a list of things that you see as you pass.

Development activity

A list sentence can be very powerful in serious writing and in speeches.

In *Gulliver's Travels*, Gulliver visits a land where horses are the intelligent rulers and men their ugly slaves.

Gulliver tells the horse king about the terrors of human warfare.

> I gave him a description of cannons, pistols, bullets, powder, swords, bayonets, battles, sieges, retreats, attacks, bombardments, sea fights; ships sunk with a thousand men, twenty thousand killed on each side; dying groans, limbs flying in the air, smoke, noise, confusion, trampling to death under horses' feet; fields strewn with carcasses left for food to dogs, and wolves, and birds of prey…

The commas hammer home the horrors of human war.

● Imagine that you were talking to the horse king. List for him some of the latest weapons and methods of fighting that are used today.

Use this opening if it helps:

I told the king about… (continue the list)

Extension

Can commas ever be exciting? They *are* sometimes, in great speeches.

On 4 June 1940, Winston Churchill, the British Prime Minister, made an important speech. It was to inspire the nation to face the possible Nazi invasion. Everything seemed hopeless but he was determined to fight on. He ended the speech with a mighty list.

> We shall go on to the end, we shall fight in France, we shall fight on the seas and oceans, we shall fight with growing confidence and growing strength in the air, we shall defend our island, whatever the cost may be, we shall fight on the beaches, we shall fight on the landing grounds, we shall fight in the fields and in the streets, we shall fight in the hills; we shall never surrender…

● Imagine your home town has been invaded by an alien species who want planet Earth for themselves.

You and the other human survivors are about to attack their spacecraft. As leader of the defence force, you need to get everyone ready for the attack.

Write the last paragraph of your speech. Use a list sentence with powerful commas to inspire your listeners.

Check your progress	LEVEL 3	I can sometimes use commas in lists
	LEVEL 4	I can use commas in lists accurately
	LEVEL 5	I can use commas accurately and effectively

This lesson will
● explain the layout and punctuation of written speech.

The punctuation and layout of written speech can look complicated, but, if you follow these guidelines, it is possible to create lively dialogue.

Getting you thinking

Look at these sentences from *Cirque du Freak* by Darren Shan.

> I saw you watching me Mr Crepsley said You gasped aloud when you first saw me Why?
>
> B-b-b-because I kn-kn-know who you a-are Steve stuttered, finding his voice
>
> I am Larten Crepsley the creepy-looking man said
>
> No Steve replied I know who you *really* are

● Can you work out what is happening here?

How does it work?

You might have worked out that this is **dialogue**. But you may have found it difficult to work out which words were their actual speech.

Glossary

dialogue: characters in a book talking together

1 It is much easier for your reader to follow what is happening if you use speech marks to show when someone is talking. Speech marks can be double ("…") or single ('…'). The actual words spoken go inside the speech marks.

'I saw you watching me' Mr Crepsley said

That's already much clearer, isn't it? Now let's add the other speech punctuation to make this a full sentence.

2 The details of who said the words go at the start, end, or sometimes the middle of the sentence. Use a comma to mark off these details. The comma goes inside the speech marks.

'I saw you watching me,' Mr Crepsley said

3 Now add a full stop at the end of the sentence.

'I saw you watching me,' Mr Crepsley said.

Now you try it

Can you do the same with the next sentence?

> B-b-b-because I kn-kn-know who you a-are Steve
> stuttered, finding his voice

- First, add the speech marks where you think they should go.
- Then add a comma and a full stop to make a complete sentence.

Development activity

Here is the rest of Steve and Mr Crepsley's conversation. We find out something very surprising!

> 'Oh?' Mr Crepsley smiled, but there was no humour in it. 'Tell me, little boy,' he sneered, 'who am I, *really*?'
>
> 'Your real name is Vur Horston,' Steve said, and Mr Crepsley's jaw dropped in astonishment. And then Steve said something else, and my jaw dropped too.
>
> '*You're a vampire*,' he said, and the silence which followed was as long as it was terrifying.

In groups of three, read this passage aloud together.

- One of you should be Mr Crepsley.
- One of you should be Steve.
- One of you should be the narrator. (The narrator is the person who tells the story.)

The person playing the narrator needs to read all the words outside the speech marks aloud.

Then, still in character, act out what you think happens next. What does Mr Crepsley say or do? How do Steve and the narrator respond?

Finally, write down a line of dialogue for each character. Use speech marks and speech punctuation. Remember to use a new line for each new speaker.

Check your progress	LEVEL 3	I can try to punctuate written speech
	LEVEL 4	I can use speech punctuation and layout fairly well
	LEVEL 5	I can use detailed speech punctuation accurately and effectively

Use bracketing commas

This lesson will
- explain how commas are used to mark off extra phrases and clauses in a sentence.

Sometimes you want to add an extra idea to a sentence. You could put this in brackets, but they are usually too heavy for the purpose. Two commas, acting like brackets, will make your writing clearer.

Getting you thinking

The extra idea or detail could be a **phrase** (a group of words without a verb).

Phrases that explain more about something need commas around them.

> Bashir Abbas, the captain, inspired the whole team. (**phrase**)

> Bashir Abbas, captaining his country for the first time, inspired the whole team. (**long phrase**)

Sometimes the extra idea comes at the beginning or end of the sentence. It will only need one comma.

> Having spent years in France, Joseph was a fluent French speaker.

> Joseph was a fluent French speaker, having spent years in France.

How does it work?

It is easy to test whether you have placed your commas correctly. If you take the extra idea away, will there still be a full sentence left?

> John grabbed the camera and, quickly switching it on, took a photo.

Take out the extra idea: quickly switching it on. The remainder makes sense on its own, so the commas were correctly placed.

Now you try it

Copy out these sentences, marking in the commas.

1 Antonio Freni a brilliant driver won the Brazilian Grand Prix.

2 Geography a subject that I hated at school is now my chief interest.

3 After finishing his homework Marco went out to play football.

4 Katya felt pleased with herself having completed the cross country run in record time.

Development activity

Extra information about people is often introduced by the word 'who'.

Meet the Brown family. Here are some facts about them:

○ Dad works at the Town Hall – tall – bald – wears glasses.

○ Mum works at the hospital – cheerful – red-haired.

○ Susie goes to nursery – aged three – chatters all day.

○ Ruff the dog was rescued from the dogs' home – friendly – very protective of Susie.

Write **four sentences** about the family, joining the facts together. Use **who** in each sentence and mark off the extra information with commas.

Level Booster

LEVEL 3

- I can use capital letters to begin sentences and full stops to end them
- I can try some speech punctuation

LEVEL 4

- I can use listing commas
- I can punctuate and set out written speech
- I can use bracketing commas

LEVEL 5

- I can use more complicated written speech
- I can use apostrophes for contraction and possession
- I can use colons and semicolons correctly

Chapter 7

AF7 Select appropriate and effective vocabulary

This chapter is going to show you how to

- Develop your descriptions by using adjectives and adverbs
- Use more imaginative vocabulary to make your ideas clearer
- Choose vocabulary that suits your topic

What's it all about?

The best words and when to use them.

This lesson will
- help you to build up your descriptions.

These pages are all about building up your descriptions with adjectives and adverbs. This will make your work more detailed and enjoyable to read.

Adjectives are used to describe nouns (things, people, places). For example, the cold wind.

Adverbs describe verbs (doing or being words). For example, the cold wind blew sharply.

Getting you thinking

Look at these two versions of a piece of writing by a student.

> I walked down the street. I was late and I knew my mum would be waiting. A boy was standing by my neighbour's car. As I opened the gate, I saw my mum looking at me through the window.

> I walked *quickly* down the *silent* street. I was *two hours* late and I knew my mum would be waiting *furiously*. A boy was standing by my neighbour's *shiny red* car. As I *hurriedly* opened the *creaking garden* gate, I saw my mum looking *angrily* at me through the window.

- Which one do you think is better? Why?
- What else could the writer have done to improve it?

Now you try it

Write out this description of a student feeling bored. Every time you find a blank, add an adjective or adverb to help the reader imagine the scene more clearly.

The first blank is filled in for you. If you get stuck, use some of the words from the vocabulary box below.

The ___scruffy___ , _____ girl was snoring _____. She woke up and there were still twenty _____ minutes to go. The _____ classroom was _____ silent. Her _____ teacher looked _____ asleep. The _____ weather made her feel worse. She looked around _____ at the _____ ticking clock.

loudly	softly	peacefully	gloomy	red	moody	moodily
mind-numbing	~~scruffy~~	dull	yawning	slowly	English
almost	desperately	longingly	patiently	young	summer
stifling	long	hot	big	miserably	totally	fast	half

Development activity

1 With a partner, use a thesaurus to make two lists of words. One should list adjectives and adverbs that can describe excitement. The other list should focus on sadness.

Excitement	Sadness

for example…

| energetic | miserable |
| suddenly | tearfully |

2 Using your lists, one of you should write about somebody who is sad, and the other about somebody who is excited. Time yourselves to write for 15 minutes, using your vocabulary bank to build up lots of imaginative descriptions. Then share your work.

Remember

Adjectives describe things (nouns) and **adverbs** describe actions (verbs).

Top tips

Try to use the five senses: sight, sound, smell, touch, taste.

Check your progress

LEVEL 3 I can use some words about sadness and excitement

LEVEL 4 I can use adjectives and adverbs that clearly describe sadness or excitement

LEVEL 5 I can use a variety of words to help the reader imagine someone sad or excited

2 Use more imaginative vocabulary to make your ideas clearer

This lesson will
- help you to describe things clearly and imaginatively.

When you are describing, try not to always pick the same words. Be imaginative and select nouns, adjectives, verbs and adverbs that will help the reader to picture exactly what you want them to see.

Getting you thinking

This extract from a Doctor Who novel called *The Monsters Inside* describes an alien emerging from its human disguise.

> The warder was just standing there. Then her hand moved to her forehead and tugged on the zipper. Blue and yellow light started to crackle and flicker from the split in her head. Her smooth complexion slid away like a rubber mask as something big and glistening and alien started to hoick itself free from its human disguise. Its head was long and broad, with wet black eyes the size of bowling balls. Its hide was knobbled and greeny-grey.
> The long arms ended in three enormous, twitching claws.

- What verbs and adjectives are used to help you picture the monster?
- How is it made to sound alien and aggressive?
- What senses does the writer use to help you imagine the scene?

Now you try it

1 Come up with as many alternatives as you can for these verbs:

To go   **To look**   **To say**

for example...

sprint	peep	yell
wander	stare	whisper

2 Share your words with your partner and discuss when it would be best to use each of your words.

For example:

I would use peep to suggest someone looking at something secretly but not wanting to be seen.

Development activity

Using nouns, verbs, adjectives and adverbs imaginatively, describe a car speeding down a street.

Choose your words carefully so that the reader can imagine

- what the car looks like
- how fast it is going
- how people react.

When you have finished, swap with your partner.

- What did you like about each other's work?
- Which words particularly helped you to imagine what was happening?

Top tips

Choose imaginative words that give the reader extra information.

BUT make sure that your alternative words still match your meaning.

Check your progress

LEVEL 3	I can think of a few good words to describe a car
LEVEL 4	I can use verbs, nouns, adjectives and adverbs to describe a car
LEVEL 5	I can choose words precisely to help the reader picture the scene

Choose vocabulary that suits your topic

This lesson will
- help you to choose descriptive words that match your topic.

You need to choose words that fit what you are writing about. You don't want to be putting creepy descriptions into a piece of work about a happy summer's day!

Getting you thinking

Look at this extract from a love story.

> Laura drifted gracefully into the room. She was beautiful. Her eyes were as green as mould and her lipstick was like a smear of blood. Her delicate, pale skin made her look like a zombie and her face was framed by greasy, golden hair. Laura's silk dress, embroidered with pretty red roses like gunshot wounds, showed off her stunning figure. Smiling at her father, her teeth shining like knives, she stamped across to meet him.

- What is wrong with it? Which words or images would you change?

Now you try it

Read this extract from a science fiction story.

> The spaceship was in orbit around Mars. Captain Matthews sat at the steering wheel and checked the map: nothing but the vastness of space. The egg timer went off, showing that his shift was over. He got up from the sofa and made his way out of the flight deck. Turning the handle, the door hissed open and Matthews walked along the carpet to his bedroom. The pretty tune of machinery echoed off the pink, metallic walls.

Using a dictionary, a thesaurus and your imagination, find an alternative for each of the red words. Try to choose vocabulary that suits a futuristic spacecraft.

Development activity

1 With a partner, decide what type (or genre) of story each of the words in the table below would suit:

- horror
- romance
- science fiction
- western
- detective story.

love	spaceship	cowboy	blood
chainsaw	crime	flowers	fingerprints
graveyard	black hole	planet	evidence
chocolates	zombie	sergeant	horse
sheriff	alien	marriage	slaughter

2 Choose one of the story types listed in question 1 and write a story opening with your partner. Try to think of lots of words and descriptions that would suit the genre of your story.

Remember

Always consider whether the words that you are choosing match what you are writing about and who you are writing to.

Level Booster

LEVEL 3

- I can use simple words correctly
- I can try to use some describing words to make my work more detailed
- I can try to use words that fit my topic

LEVEL 4

- I can use more difficult words correctly, making some imaginative vocabulary choices
- I can use some describing words to make my work more detailed and enjoyable for the reader
- I can choose words that fit my topic

LEVEL 5

- I can use a range of more difficult words correctly
- I can use a range of describing words to make my work interesting and to develop specific ideas
- I can use a range of words that fit my topic to achieve my purpose

Chapter 8

AF8 Use correct spelling

This chapter is going to show you how to

- Secure your basic spellings
- Spell -ly adverbs

What's it all about?

Securing your spelling.

This lesson will
- show you how to spell plurals
- show you how to spell words containing ie and ei
- show you how to spell words that start with silent letters.

These pages are all about learning to spell correctly.

How does it work?

Plurals

When there is more than one of something, it is called a **plural**.
There are three simple rules to help you spell plurals correctly.

1 For most words, simply <u>add the letter 's'</u>. For example

  dog ⟶ dogs
  house ⟶ houses

However, there are two times when this rule doesn't apply…

2 Words that <u>end in an E sound</u> are different.
Take off the 'y' and add 'ies' in its place. For example

  baby ⟶ babies
  fairy ⟶ fairies

3 Words that <u>end with a SH sound</u> and words that <u>end with a letter 's'</u> are also different. Instead of just adding an 's', add an 'es'. For example

  dish ⟶ dishes
  wish ⟶ wishes

> **Top tips**
>
> You don't need to change all words that end with a letter 'y' to 'ies', only those that end with an E sound. For example, tray becomes trays, not traies.

Now you try it

Use the rules above to help you turn these words into plurals:

  pass month cat mile building library year flash bucket face

How does it work?

Spelling words with 'ie' or 'ei'

Here is a spelling rule that you can use most of the time:
i before e, except after c, but only when the sound is E.

For example:
- grief has i before e because it is an E sound
- height has e before i because it is not an E sound
- perceive has e before i because, although it is an E sound, it comes straight after a c.

Now you try it

Use the rules above to help you decide which word in each list is spelled incorrectly. Check your answers in the dictionary.

1 Fiend, Nieghbour, Shriek
2 Chief, Recieve, Piece
3 Ceiling, Brief, Theif
4 Believe, Relief, Wieght

How does it work?

Silent letters at the start of a word

Some words are difficult to spell because they contain silent letters, so you cannot work out the spelling by saying the word out loud. For example, the words 'ghost' and 'school' both have a silent 'h'.

Now you try it

Using a dictionary and three headings, make a list of words that begin…

‘Kn’ (a silent k)   ‘Wh’ (a silent h)   ‘Rh’ (a silent h)

For example…

Kneel   Where   Rhyme

Development activity

Can you correct the spellings? At the end, check your answers with a dictionary.

Last knight I saw two cattes sitting in my garden. I now this sounds wierd, and I bet you don't beleive me, but it was as if these two animales were watching me. Their eys followed me and they sat there like angry rinos, wieghing up wether to attack me or not. Then they shreiked like strange babys and raced away.

Top tips

Keep a dictionary with you when you are writing.

Read regularly: the more you see words, the more you will spell them correctly.

Check your progress

LEVEL 3 | I can spell short basic words correctly
LEVEL 4 | I can spell most basic words including ie words and plurals
LEVEL 5 | I can spell basic words, including ie words, plurals and words that sound the same

83

This lesson will
- show you how to spell adverbs.

A key skill at Level 4 is being able to spell adverbs correctly.

How does it work?

Adverbs are words that describe a verb.

He ate his food quickly

ate is the verb   the adverb describes *how* he ate.

Notice that the adverb 'quickly' is originally an adjective with -ly added onto the end.

Now you try it

Copy out this paragraph, completing the spellings of the underlined adverbs.

The car came <u>sudden</u> around the bend, racing <u>mad</u> down the road. People got out of its way <u>quick</u>, screaming <u>loud</u>. Children watched <u>excited</u> as the car veered <u>wild</u> across the path before coming <u>slow</u> to a halt. The door opened <u>gradual</u>. A man got out, smiling <u>broad</u>, then walked <u>silent</u> away.

Development activity

Copy down this spelling rule:

When spelling most adverbs, simply add -ly onto the end of the original adjective. For example, quietly = quiet + ly.

The adverb 'quietly' would be used to describe someone doing something in a quiet way.

However, some adverbs are spelled in a slightly different way.

1 Using a dictionary, find out how to spell the adverbs that would describe…

- eating in a hungry way ('He ate _____')
- someone laughing in a scary way ('He laughed _____')
- a girl smiling in a pretty way ('She smiled _____')

Once you have found your spellings, write a rule to remind yourself how to spell adverbs when the original adjective ends in a 'y'.

2 Using a thesaurus, make a list of adverbs that you could use to describe the following verbs. Spend five minutes on each verb.

Move   Look   Say

For example…

swiftly   nastily   rudely

3 As an extension, check the following adverbs. If they are spelled incorrectly, change them. You can use a dictionary if you need to. If you don't know what some of the words mean, use the dictionary to find out as this will help you to improve your vocabulary.

beautifuly	dizzily	foolishily
craftyly	doubtfully	strangely
cunningly	evilly	tearfully

Remember

The English language is not always logical! Sometimes there are exceptions to a rule. Always check a word in the dictionary if you are unsure of how to spell it.

When you've finished, share with your partner and check that you have both got them right.

Check your progress

LEVEL 3	I can spell some -ly adverbs
LEVEL 4	I can spell most -ly adverbs
LEVEL 5	I can spell a variety of adverbs

85

Level Booster

LEVEL 3

- I can spell some familiar words
- I can spell words that are spelled as they sound

LEVEL 4

- I can spell most familiar words and plurals
- I can spell most adverbs with an -ly ending

LEVEL 5

- I can spell familiar words and some more complex words
- I can use prefixes and suffixes to spell the openings and endings of words correctly

Teacher Guide

Where the final task of the double-page section is substantial enough to provide a snapshot of students' progress, this has been marked as an **APP opportunity**.

Each double-page section ends with a **Check your progress** box. This offers a levelled checklist against which students can self- or peer-assess their final piece of writing from the **Development** or, occasionally, **Now you try it** section.

The end of chapter **Level Booster** is a less task-specific checklist of the skills students need to master to reach Level 3, 4 and 5. It can be used to help students see the level they are working at currently and to visualise what they need to do to make progress.

To the Teacher

The general aim of these books is the practical and everyday application of **Assessment for Learning (AfL)**: to ensure every child knows how they are doing and what they need to do to improve. The specific aim is to support **APP (Assessing Pupils' Progress)**: the 'periodic' view of progress by teacher and learner.

The books empower the student by modelling the essential skills needed at each level, and by allowing them to practise and then demonstrate independently what they know and can do across every reading and writing (APP) strand. They help the teacher by providing opportunities to gather and review secure evidence of day-to-day progress in each **Assessment Focus (AF)**. Where appropriate (and especially at lower levels) the books facilitate teacher **scaffolding** of such learning and assessment.

The series offers exercises and examples that we hope will not only help students add descriptive power and nuance to their vocabulary but also expand the grammatical constructions they can access and use: above all, the ability to write and read in sentences (paragraphs, texts) – to think consciously in complete thoughts. We aim at fuller, more complex self-expression – developing students' ability to express themselves simply or with complexity and the sense to choose when each is apt.

Each AF is a provisional isolation of various emphases, to be practised and mastered before bringing it back to the real reading and writing (of whole texts) in which all these – suitably polished – skills can be applied.

Gareth Calway

Series Editor

1 Bring your writing to life

Getting you thinking

Read the two speeches aloud or ask students to perform them.

How does it work?

Draw out the following points with students:

The second version would **do the job** much better than the first example. It would make the players sit up in their seats.

The first example is **too brief**. It doesn't explain what went wrong (not enough balls in the box).

The language is **lively and detailed** in the second example. It makes comparisons that are striking and funny – and scary!

Finally, the speech **builds up a number of points** (you've done badly, you need to do better in the second half, get out there now and score some goals).

You may also want to draw attention to other aspects of the language: the writer's use of alliteration (in the first line), exclamation marks, the imperative and questions.

2 Use real details in your writing

Getting you thinking

Explain that this is Orwell's account of a real event: watching a man being hanged.

Read the passage aloud to students at least once to ensure they have understood it.

Ask them to tell you how they think Orwell felt about this event.

Ask them to tell you what really struck them about Orwell's account. Which one detail sticks in their minds?

How does it work?

Orwell was an eyewitness to this real event. Almost every word and sentence seems proof of this.

With students

- Look at the description of the prisoner's **appearance**: his 'bare brown back'.
- Look at the description of his **movement**: 'he walked clumsily with his bound arms'.
- Most importantly, look at the **key detail** Orwell picks out: 'he stepped slightly aside to avoid a puddle'.

Why is this detail so striking? Why would a man care about getting his feet wet when he is about to die? Could Orwell have made this detail up if he hadn't seen it?

The detail of the prisoner avoiding the puddle would have been very hard to invent had Orwell not actually seen it. It is such a small observation and yet has such a huge impact.

You want students to understand that details from their own real experience can be very powerful, even when writing fiction – a made-up story.

Now you try it

Explain that they are making up a story now, imagining that they saw a bike being stolen. However, you want them to try to think of details from their own experience – of a bike they know or perhaps a crime they have witnessed – that could make their account more vivid.

Development

Help students to run the role-play. Instruct the 'police officer' to ask their partner questions about what they saw. They could start by thinking of three questions, but then press for more details to test the witness' story. Think TV police drama!

3 Choose and plan the right content

Now you try it

1 Model how this text answers the original questions.

Big Issue. Buy the *Big Issue*! Read this week's exciting interview with the Kaiser Chiefs. Only £2.40 and all to help the homeless. The ideal read for your shopping coffee break. Get rid of any bits of loose change – I don't mind taking the weight for you! Not interested, madam? Well, have a nice day anyway. Thank you, sir. It's people like you that make it all worthwhile.

Explain to students that if their seller actually took the spiel onto the streets, they would find themselves improving it further. But you need **a good plan** to even get that far.

2 *Now write a similar plan for a different sales pitch.*

Encourage students to cover each bullet in their plan but also to 'lose' anything **at the planning stage** that isn't going to help sell the trainers.

Students could swap their work with a partner here, and check the final pitch against the plan.

4 Choose the best words

Explain to students that often if you choose the right noun or verb, they will do the describing for you. If you want to call a teenager (noun) by the adjective 'fashionable' you can. But choose a noun like 'dude' or 'babe' and the job's already done.

Now you try it

Read the first passage aloud. Ask for students' opinions on this piece of writing. Did they find it exciting? Have they ever seen or held a snake? Does this paragraph express what it felt like?

Show students that the words don't do the subject justice. We need more words for **colours, movement, sound, sensations,** *feelings*.

Then read the Levertov poem at least once with students, asking them to pick out words and phrases they like that sound *snaky*.

How does it work?

Draw out in discussion what the poet has done, asking students to share their chosen words and phrases. For example:

- The second writer chooses words and phrases that have **movement, sound** and **colour**.
- The poem focuses on sensations: the snake's weight, its hiss, its whispering movement, its dryness. We feel with the poet what it is like to hold a snake.

- Read the phrase 'The whispering silver of your dryness' aloud to students and ask them to comment on its *sound*. What do all the hissing 's' sounds remind them of?

- Both writers describe with nouns. But the second writer makes her poem more alive by using **extended noun phrases** like 'The whispering silver of your dryness'. Explain that an extended noun phrase is a group of words that does the job of a noun in the sentence: they name something, but they name it in a descriptive way.

- The -ing words – pulsing and whispering – describe the snake with adjectives made from verbs. These -ing words (present participles) suggest **movement**.

Development

Explain that the word choices here are very dull, and sometimes just wrong. Snakes aren't slimy for a start – the fear makes you feel they're slimy perhaps, but snakes are warm and dry.

Ask students if the phrases 'really scared' and 'relieved' express the poet's intense emotions well.

Guide students towards replacing **noun plus adjective** with a **descriptive noun**, and **verb plus adverb** with a **descriptive verb**, as they rewrite the poem. For instance, 'Hit hard' could be a descriptive verb like 'hammered'.

5 Grab the reader's attention

How does it work?

- The headline is the **hook** that sells the newspaper. It must **grab** the reader's attention.

- The sub-headline draws the reader in further.

- The first paragraph **holds the interest** and expands it. It must answer the key questions: **who is involved – and what happened?** It sums up the story.

Explain that like a newspaper headline, the first sentence of a fiction story must **grab the reader's attention**. Once we're **hooked**, the story builds up to a bigger excitement at the very end, keeping us in suspense until then.

The essential point for students to grasp is that a fiction story – indeed any text – needs an arresting opening, like a newspaper headline.

As an extension, explore with students how newspaper articles and fiction stories work differently *after* their opening. A newspaper article starts with its most exciting point, or the paper stays on the shelf. It gives away the 'story' or the 'ending' in a way that a fiction story would not.

Now you try it

Draw out why Kafka's opening is more exciting. Explain that all of the other information in the first version will have to be given at some point. But none of it did the job of **grabbing the attention**. At the start, all that is needed is to **hook** and then **hold** the reader.

Development

As an extension activity, ask students who have mastered **grabbing** the reader's attention to have a go at **holding** it:

1 Select the opening you gave the highest grab value. Write the opening paragraph of a story for this opening.

2 Check these in your groups. How did your openings compare for 'grab' and 'hold' of interest?

Chapter 2 AF2 Produce texts which are appropriate to task, reader and purpose

1 Decide what type of writing you are being asked to do

How does it work?

The writer makes some valid points about the holiday and makes it clear what he or she would like the reader to do.

But is it really suitable as a formal letter of complaint?

Did students notice how the writer has

- used words such as 'pants', 'rubbish' and 'fab' which are not suitable for a formal letter

- included comments that are not relevant to the task ('always a positive' and 'The weather was really hot')

- ended the letter in a rather rude way.

As you discuss the points, ask students to suggest more formal-sounding words that the writer

could have used to express dissatisfaction: for instance, 'awful', 'horrific' or 'disappointing'.

Ask students how the writer should have ended the letter. For example, 'The hotel was not up to standard and I would like a full refund.'

Development

1 Explain to students that when we decide to write something we need to think about our purpose: why we are writing. There is often a form of writing – or a range of forms – best suited to this purpose. However, there are also forms that are unsuitable.

2 This activity is about planning how to approach a writing task. Students do not need to write the article.

Guide students to think about what 'ingredients' are normally found in newspaper articles. For example, a headline that captures the reader's attention; often a picture; text must be written in short paragraphs and set out in columns. Students might want to think about interviewing someone – a teacher, a fellow student or a parent – and including their opinion in the article.

Extension

You could get students to think further about why and what we write by setting them this exercise for homework:

Carry out a survey!

Your family, teachers and friends will do a lot of different writing activities in a single week.

Investigate the different types of writing they have carried out and for each one find out what their purpose was.

Or, keep a record yourself. You might be surprised at how many different sorts of writing you do in a single week. For example, you may have

- written job applications
- updated blogs or social networking pages
- sent emails or letters.

For each task say what the purpose was for writing.

2 Write in the correct style for a task

Getting you thinking

Read the text aloud together. Ask students to work in pairs to answer the question, finding three strengths or three weaknesses in the text.

How does it work?

You could say that this extract is not very persuasive because the writer hasn't managed to write in the correct style.

The paragraph makes Oundle sound anything but attractive!

Did students notice that

- the writer uses very dull **adjectives** such as old, small and cheap
- the sentences all **start** in the same boring way: 'It has', 'There is'.

The writer could have made the text more persuasive by

- using a more enticing selection of **descriptive vocabulary**
- **talking directly to the reader** as 'you' and asking questions
- starting sentences in different ways.

Now you try it

Draw out in discussion what makes this text more successful:

- The text starts directly with an appeal to the reader. The **rhetorical question** makes the reader think.

- The writer lists some of the activities in **groups of three** to make it sound like there is lots on offer.
- The writer starts each sentence in an engaging way, by **posing questions** or beginning with a verb like 'Stroll' which makes Reading sound like a pleasant place to spend time in.

Development

If stuck, students could describe a place they have visited or somewhere they've always wanted to visit.

Before students start writing, ask them to consider the following points:

1 **Think about who your audience is.** I need to appeal to people who are thinking of taking a trip somewhere new.

2 **Try and appeal directly to your reader** by talking to the reader as 'you' or by asking questions.

3 **Think about the characteristics of this type of writing:** for example, plenty of attractive descriptions and interesting verbs.

4 **Persuasive texts are very positive.** I need to ensure that I highlight the best things about my area.

Keep the checklist on the board as they write.

When students have finished, they should swap their work with a partner and give each other feedback, using the checklist above as a starting point.

3 Use different techniques to interest the reader

Getting you thinking

Read each scary story extract aloud at least once to students.

How does it work?

Talk through what is happening in each extract. Ask students to imagine what might happen next.

Did they notice how each extract tries to **build up tension**?

Point out how the writer of Extract A uses

- a **long sentence** to introduce the idea that something is in the room
- **short sentences**, such as the one word sentence, 'Silence.', to increase tension.

Explain how Extract B is written

- in the **first person**, using 'I', as if you were the narrator.

Tension is built up slowly in Extract A; nothing much actually happens but we feel worried about what is going to happen to the boy.

In Extract B, the man and the woman seem to have more control over what is happening than the boy, closing the door and steering the boy. This increases our tension and makes them sound slightly sinister.

Point out that both writers include a wealth of detail and vivid vocabulary to help us feel as if we are in the scene. Explain that the first writer has used a **simile**, 'his eyes were as wide as an owls', to show how scared and alert the boy is.

Development

Encourage students to use **two** of the techniques below to bring their passage to life for the reader. Explain that their writing will benefit more from developing a couple of techniques well than from trying to include everything.

- Include a **simile** to bring a scene or person to life by comparing it to something else using the words 'like' or 'as'.
- Use some very **short sentences** for dramatic effect or **longer sentences** to set the scene.
- Use **action words (verbs)** to build up tension.
- Think about giving objects human characteristics (**personification**) as when the door 'sighed open' in the first extract.
- Decide whether you will write in the **first person** using 'I' or the **third person** using 'she' or 'he'.

Keep this list on the board while students are writing.

4 Develop a viewpoint in your writing

How does it work?

The writer makes his viewpoint really clear by

- giving examples of how uniforms 'crush the individual spirit'
- using a personal memory to support his point of view
- signalling his view with the phrase, 'The main reason'.

Now you try it

- *Rewrite the paragraph to develop a clear viewpoint.*

Model and encourage students to use **one or more** of these techniques in their paragraph:

- **Using the first person 'I'**: 'I believe that this is incredibly important…'
- **Making your opinions clear to the reader with a judgement**: 'This is not the case.'

- **Giving personal examples to support your ideas.**
- **Signalling to the reader that you are right and that they should agree with you**: 'I'm sure that you remember how hard and uncomfortable your school uniform was and you will agree with me when I say…'

Keep this checklist on the board as they write.

Extension

Play students a news clip which shows the presenter interviewing someone or asking for their opinion. Students should make a note of all the different phrases the interviewee uses to make their viewpoint obvious to the listener. Can they use any of these phrases to improve their own piece of writing?

1 Organise your writing

How does it work?

Ask students what would happen if you followed these vague instructions? Draw out from them that you'd probably end up burning some ingredients and undercooking others. You might well end up with food poisoning too!

These instructions could be much more detailed and organised in a more logical way.

Point out to students that a lot of information is missing, such as

- a heading telling the user what they are cooking
- a list of ingredients and quantities
- how many people the recipe would feed.

Many key stages in the process are forgotten about.

- Should you cook all the ingredients at once, or in stages?
- What temperature should you cook them at? For how long?

Now you try it

Use this activity to encourage students to plan, read and redraft their work. Ask students to swap their first draft with a partner and make suggestions for improvements. Have they missed anything out? This can be added in the final version.

2 Writing a clear introduction and conclusion

Now you try it

Once students have drafted their work, encourage them to share it with a partner and take suggestions for redrafting.

Remind students that their conclusion should summarise their argument and include summative words and phrases. Do they need to add any of these?

3 Use linking words and phrases

Getting you thinking

You will need to go through the list of linking words or phrases with students, explaining what each one means and modelling how it could be used (including placing a comma after the word or phrase where necessary).

How does it work?

Draw out that the phrase 'For example' links the two sentences together as the first sentence tells us what the person is feeling and the second goes on to explain, using an example, why they feel this way.

4 Make sure your writing stays organised

Getting you thinking

Read the article aloud. Model for students what the key point of paragraph one is and then ask them to discuss the questions.

How does it work?

Feed back students' ideas, drawing out the following points:

- The second paragraph tells us that Sonic the Hedgehog came top of the list of most popular games, while the third paragraph **develops** this by detailing what games were lower on the list.
- The article stays focused on the topic of popular computer games throughout.
- Notice how the concluding paragraph links back to the second paragraph. They both mention the London Games Festival which carried out this survey.

Now you try it

Draw attention to repeated words such as 'popular' (paragraphs one and two); 'Sonic' (paragraphs three and four); 'Sega' (paragraphs four and five).

Development

1 *Re-draft your work, this time making sure you have used all the techniques to improve your writing.*

Ask students to check that each paragraph links to or develops from the previous paragraph.

Encourage them to use linking phrases to make one paragraph flow from the last. For example, '**As well as** fantastic lyrics, the track ...' (See the previous spread on linking words.)

If students need further support, you could write this paragraph plan on the board and work through it with them:

Paragraph 1

Write about great parties and what makes them great, especially music.

> ***Great parties need great music.*** *Everyone knows when a great song is on because...*

Paragraph 2

Say what the best song for a party is and who it is by.

> *The best song,* ***therefore,*** *for a party is...*

Paragraph 3

Give reasons why it's the best song.

> ***This is because...***

Paragraph 4

Sum up your main points about the song.

> *So, if you are at a terrible party then....*

5 Present your work effectively on the page

For this lesson, you will need to have to hand a range of suitable magazines for students to look through. Ask students to bring in their own choice of mag too.

Getting you thinking

Emphasise that students don't need to read the whole article – they are primarily thinking about how it *looks* on the page (how it has been set out and what features the designer or editor has chosen to include).

How does it work?

Explain to students that to attract the casual browser's eye, magazines use

- **pictures** to show the reader who or what the article is about
- **headings** to tell the reader what the article is about and to make them want to find out more
- **colour** to make the page look attractive
- **different fonts** to attract the reader's attention and add interest.

Ask students who they think the article is aimed at. (Children? Teenagers? The elderly?) What tells them this? (The fonts? The images chosen? The use of simple language and short paragraphs?)

You may want to explore with students why particular background colours or designs are chosen. Here they pick up the colours of the central image. Sometimes the designer chooses colours that reflect the subject of the article. For instance, an article about a footballer might use the colours of their team's kit, or green to represent the football pitch.

Development

Explain to students that when it is their turn to be interviewed they will need to decide what makes them famous. If stuck, they can pretend to be their favourite – or least favourite – celebrity.

Remind them that their heading should tell the reader what the 'story' is – what the article is about.

How might the pictures, colours and design reflect the content or subject of their article?

You may want to allow students to use the internet to find pictures of their celebrity to include in their mock-up magazine page.

Extension

Ask students to actually draft out a short article, using the questions and answers from their role-play. It should follow the format of the *Mizz* article.

1 Recognise paragraphs and the topic sentence

Tell students that when you write by hand, you indent the first line of your paragraph. When you write on the computer, leave one line-space between paragraphs.

Model indenting the first line of a paragraph or leaving a line between paragraphs.

Development

If students are struggling you could give them these ideas for four sentences:

- why does he keep the tigers?
- where does he keep them?
- what does he train them to do?
- any accidents?

2 Use supporting and ending sentences

Getting you thinking

Model how supporting and ending sentences are used.

How does it work?

Explain to students that

- The **topic sentence** is the most important sentence in the paragraph. It introduces the idea or topic that the paragraph is going to be about.
- The **supporting sentences** tell you more about the idea or topic in the paragraph.

- The **ending sentence** completes the idea or topic and ends the paragraph.

Now you try it

You'll need coloured pens or pencils for this activity.

Development

Ask students to share their mime with another group. Each group should perform their mime, and the other group should take notes and make suggestions about how they could improve it.

3 Develop your Paragraphs

Getting you thinking

Model the three types of paragraph development with students.

How does it work?

Show students how in the first example the paragraph is brought to life by using supporting sentences suggesting how rough the sea actually was. The reader can picture exactly what is happening.

Now you try it

Remind students to look back at the three examples to see how a paragraph can be developed by 1) supporting sentences, 2) drawing comparisons, 3) providing reasons.

Development

Encourage students to redraft their diary entry on the computer using their IT skills.

4 Arrange paragraphs logically and make links between them

How does it work?

Explain to students that if a piece of writing is written well it should be easy to rearrange jumbled paragraphs, as most stories follow a sequence. There will also normally be links made between one paragraph and the next.

The order is: **c, b, d, a**.

Point out **links** such as the mention of the oldies in paragraphs **b** and **d** or the buildings in paragraphs **c** and **b**. These help us to determine the order, as do linking words such as 'Later'.

95

Now you try it

3 Ask students to make a thought tunnel for Anna. As she walks through the tunnel, whisper what she might think, feel and want to know.

To create a thought tunnel, the class need to form two straight lines facing each other. They touch fingertips and the person going through the tunnel needs to stoop and make his way through the tunnel.

Development

As an extension, students could swap their work with another pair. See whether they can place the paragraphs in the correct order. If their order is different, discuss the reasons why. Can they can come up with an agreed order?

5 Using paragraphs when writing letters

How does it work?

Explore with students how each paragraph in the letter introduces a new topic. Each new paragraph describes a different aspect of Gemma's life in East Anglia.

Each paragraph also has a topic sentence, supporting sentences and an ending sentence.

With one paragraph, model finding the topic and supporting sentences.

Development

1 *Write a letter to a friend telling the friend all about a strange experience you have had recently. Use about five or six paragraphs. What happened, what did you do?*

This is the synoptic activity for the chapter so students should draw on everything they have learned in the other units. It may be helpful to put this list on the board as a reminder while they write:

Remember to

● use a new paragraph every time there is a new incident, topic, place, time or person.

● make links between one paragraph and the next

● indent the first line of each paragraph or, if you are using the computer, leave a line space between paragraphs

● set out your letter following the format of Gemma's letter.

Chapter 5 AF5 Vary sentences for clarity, purpose and effect

1 Check that simple sentences are correct

Getting you thinking

You will need recording devices for this activity (computer, tape recorders or, if appropriate, mobile phones).

This activity is designed to help students understand that they naturally use these subject / verb sentence structures all the time in speech. Grammar describes the way we communicate; it isn't something alien they need to learn.

Explain to students that although we do not normally speak in full sentences, they should still be able to find the basic subject / verb structures in what they said. This is how we think in English.

How does it work?

You may want to explain to students that there are two parts of verbs that are not complete by themselves. They are called **participles**:

> **going** (present participle)
> **gone** (past participle).

You cannot build sentences around these on their own. They are too weak.

For instance:

> Fatima going to the shops.

> My father gone to have his hair cut.

These do not sound right. Participles need little **helping** (or **auxiliary**) **verbs** to make them complete.

> Fatima <u>is</u> going to the shops. ('is going' is the complete verb)

> My father <u>has</u> gone to have his hair cut. ('has gone' is the complete verb)

Development

Can you do the same with the last three lines?

● *First remove the dashes and commas.*
● *Then add the words you think are missing.*

Mostly the verbs are there but the subjects are missing. Students will need to add these and any missing verbs to make full, simple sentences. Model this for them with the first sentence, given as an example.

When students have finished, ask them to underline the subject and verb in each sentence to check it works.

2 Use simple sentences for effect

Getting you thinking

Read the passage aloud to students and draw attention to those final two short sentences in your reading. Ask students which sentences were most striking.

How does it work?

Simple sentences do not have to be dull. They can be useful for dramatic moments like these in stories.

Here short paragraphs and short sentences express the shock effect of finding the dead body.

Discuss with students how short sentences slow down the pace of a text as we read and can therefore be really useful for emphasis – drawing the reader's attention to a shock or surprise.

Development

It might help to photocopy the original fire alarm passage for students and then ask them to cross out any information that is not relevant.

Model the decisions made in cutting the first example sentence and turning it into two bullet points.

You will need to explain how command sentences (or the imperative) work.

● We use **command sentences** to give instructions. These short sentences miss out the implied subject ('you') and just use the verb.
● For example: 'Do what I say', 'Come here', 'Listen to me'.

3 Use compound sentences with conjunctions

How does it work?

And, but, or, yet, either/or, neither/nor are called coordinating conjunctions. They join together ideas of equal strength.

Explain to students that coordinating conjunctions allow you to combine ideas, avoid wasting words and make your ideas flow more smoothly.

Model for students how conjunctions work. Compare this compound sentence to a set of sentences without conjunctions.

Ivan got into the car, drove to his mother's house, had dinner with her <u>and</u> returned home late.

Ivan got into the car. He drove to his mother's house. He had dinner with her. He returned home late.

Explain to students that all of the sentences in the second example are correct but they are repetitive and hard to read smoothly. Conjunctions can make a difference!

Development

In *A Farewell to Arms*, the American novelist Ernest Hemingway wrote about his experience as an ambulance driver on the Italian Front during the First World War. As he and his friends eat their rations in a trench dugout, it is hit by a shell.

Read the passage aloud to students and explain the context to them.

The short sentences and conjunctions are perfect to catch the confusion and sudden horror of the shell explosion.

Draw out responses from students about the passage. Which sentence do they find most powerful?

1 *Imagine you are walking along a tow-path on a rainy day, when you accidentally slip and fall into the river. You are desperately trying to stay afloat and reach the bank. You have also injured yourself badly in the fall.*

Use a series of simple and compound sentences,

*like Hemingway's, to describe the confusion of
what is happening.*

You may want to help students complete the
writing task by providing some sentence
openings on the board to get them started:

*Suddenly, I slipped in the mud and…
I felt… and…
There was blood… and…
I tried to… but…
I could neither… nor…*

4 Try out complex sentences

Getting you thinking

This lesson is about **complex sentences**. You may
feel it is appropriate to tell students more about
the grammatical construction of these sentences.

Explain that some complex sentences contain
two (or more) **clauses**. A clause is a group of
words which contains a **subject** and a **verb**.

Unlike in **compound sentences**, which join
clauses of equal strength, in complex sentences
one clause (the **main clause**) is usually more
important than the other (the **subordinate
clause**). The subordinate clause just adds extra
information to the main clause.

They couldn't stop talking, **when** they finally met.
    main clause   subordinate clause

We use **subordinating conjunctions** to join the
subordinate clause(s) to the main clause. **When,**

if and **because** are the most likely subordinating
conjunctions for students at this level to use.

How does it work?

Ask students to feed back their complete
sentences from the first activity. Model how they
could rearrange their sentences to put the
subordinate clause (the extra information) at the
start and middle of the sentence.

Development

Model a couple of sentences using these other
subordinating conjunctions, to show students
how they work. For example:

> **As long as** *you don't tell anyone the secret, your
> friend will always trust you.*

> **Unless** *you are a supermodel in waiting, choose
> clothes that suit your body shape.*

Chapter 6 AF6 Write with technical accuracy of syntax and punctuation in phrases, clauses and sentences

---

1 Use commas in lists

Getting you thinking

Read the final passage from Dickens aloud to
students first and ask them what the rhythm of
the sentence reminds them of. Then ask them to
read it aloud themselves in pairs, pausing for
breath at each comma.

How does it work?

You may want to note that although he could
have used semicolons to divide the items,
Dickens prefers commas which make the
description move more quickly.

Extension

You may want to draw attention to the function
of commas in speeches which allow the speaker a
pause for breath.

June 1940 was a dark time in European history.
The Nazis under Adolf Hitler had conquered most
of Western Europe, including France. The British
army had been driven to the Channel coast at
Dunkirk. Britain stood alone, awaiting the
onslaught of the German air force and possible
invasion.

Explain the dramatic historical context of
Churchill's speech, then read the speech extract
aloud to students, emphasising the commas and
the final semicolon.

Explain to students that the commas are part of
the power here, providing light pauses for breath
between the vivid images, helping the build up to
the great final promise, with a heavier pause
(shown by a semicolon) before it.

2 Punctuate and set out written speech

How does it work?

Model placing the commas and speech marks for students. Show them how the 'said / says' identification can be placed in different positions within a sentence.

Ensure students understand the difference between opening and closing speech marks.

Explain to students that when you write a whole conversation, you need to

- start a new line for each new speaker
- **indent** the first line of each new speaker's words.

    'I am Larten Crepsely,' the creepy-looking man said.

    'No,' Steve replied. 'I know who you *really* are.'

Once your reader knows who is speaking, there is no need to keep repeating the 'he says' and 'she says' bits.

You may like to note to students that short forms like <u>didn't</u>, <u>I'm</u>, <u>haven't</u> are rightly used in speech. Explain that they would not normally use them in more formal writing, like essays, letters or reports.

Development

Explain to students that dialogue makes a story lively and interesting. It also tells us more about the characters. We learn what they are like from **what they say** and **how they say it**. For instance, we learn that Mr Crepsley is a 'creepy-looking man'. We can tell Steve is scared of him because he stutters when he speaks to him.

Tell students that they can improve their dialogue by adding more description to the **says** and **said** sections outside the speech marks.

Help students to write a line of dialogue for their character:

- They can begin by noting down something they said in the role play.
- Next help them to write this line up by adding speech marks.
- Do they want to add any extra information about how their character acted, looked or sounded? Help them to put these words inside the speech marks. Could they use a more interesting word than 'said' to describe how the line was spoken?
- Finally, insert the comma inside the speech marks (or question mark / exclamation mark if more appropriate) and a full stop at the end of the sentence.

3 Use bracketing commas

Development

You may want to explain to students how to use

   who   whom   which   that

These are called **relative pronouns**. **Who/whom/that** apply to people, while **that/which** apply to **things**.

Explain that a sentence with a relative clause allows you to escape the boring repetition of subject names or things.

   Wen Fu won the race. Wen Fu was an outstanding runner.

   ▼

   Wen Fu, who was an outstanding runner, easily won the race.

Tell them to place the relative clause or pronoun just after the person or thing to which it applies to avoid mistakes.

My father helped the homeless man whom I admire for his kindness. (✗ Wrong: it's the father who is kind.)

My father, whom I admire for his kindness, helped the homeless man. (✓ Relative pronoun correctly placed.)

It's easy to get **who** and **whom** confused. Students just need to remember that **whom** replaces **him**, **her** or **it** in the subordinate clause.

   Alice was wearing **her** new coat. I saw **her** in the High Street.

   Alice, **whom** I saw in the High Street, was wearing her new coat.

   Tamer Mustafa is now a famous man. I knew **him** at school.

   Tamer Mustafa, **whom** I knew at school, is now a famous man.

Extension

Clauses which tell you about people or things can be a particular problem. Do you use bracketing commas or not?

If extra information is being added to a sentence that already stands on its own, use them.

The Johnsons, **whose house you are renting**, are living in Germany for a year.

extra

These are called **non-defining clauses**.

If the sentence would be very different if you took the extra out, then do not use bracketing commas.

The teacher who inspired me taught art.

(The teacher taught art would mean much less)

These are called **defining clauses**.

Chapter 7 AF7 Select appropriate and effective vocabulary

1 Develop your descriptions by using adjectives and adverbs

How does it work?

As you feed back students' responses, draw attention to the words in italics: the adjectives and adverbs that have been added to improve the piece to a Level 4.

Explain that the first version gets across what is happening. However, the second version is much more interesting to read! It includes more detail by using adjectives and adverbs.

These describing words

- help you picture what is happening in your head
- tell us more about how the boy and his mother are feeling.

Development

An extension activity for students who finish early:

Play a describing game with your partner. Come up with as many adjectives as you can for each of these nouns:

Chocolate, icicle, glass, smoke, night, dragon, fairground, fire.

Take it in turns. If you get stuck and can't think of one, your partner wins that noun and you can move onto another.

2 Use more imaginative vocabulary

Getting you thinking

Read the extract aloud and ask students to tell you how the description makes them feel.

How does it work?

Point out to students how the writer uses

- adjectives to help you to picture the size of the monster (broad, long, enormous) and the texture of its skin (glistening, wet, knobbled)
- verbs to show the effort and energy involved in this grisly transformation (hoick, tugged, slid).

Now you try it

A more challenging extension task would be for students to think about the different meanings of synonyms. The aim is for them to understand that some words are more appropriate in certain

contexts because they have a specific meaning:

1 *In your pairs, using a thesaurus, find alternatives for these adjectives:*

dry, wet, hot, cold, scary, calm, tired, rude, bright, pale.

With the help of a dictionary, decide what extra meaning each of your alternatives has and when it would be best to use each one.

For example: *dry = dehydrated, arid*

I'd use dehydrated to describe someone suffering from thirst

I'd use arid to describe a desert where there is no water

As an extension, try to use your favourite new word in a sentence.

Development

Remind students what nouns, verbs, adjectives and adverbs are, modelling on the board an example of each that is related to the task.

Nouns are naming words for people, places and things (**Bob**, **Spain**, **the table**).

Verbs are doing or being words denoting actions or states (he **runs**, she **is**).

Adjectives describe nouns (the **cold** wind).

Adverbs describe verbs (he moved **swiftly**).

3 Choose vocabulary that suits your topic

Getting you thinking

Read the extract aloud to students first, to increase the element of surprise.

How does it work?

The opening sounds like a conventional love story with words such as 'gracefully' and 'beautiful'. However, the writer then makes some unusual word and image choices.

Explain to students that in a love story you wouldn't normally

- use phrases like 'green as mould' or 'smear of blood' to describe an attractive girl
- call her a 'zombie'
- use similes such as 'like gunshot wounds' or 'like knives' to describe her appearance
- describe her hair as 'greasy'.

You could also mention that the girl sounds too aggressive: 'drift' is a good word to describe her movements but 'stamped' isn't. Similarly, referring to 'daggers' and 'gunshot wounds' makes her sound like a monster, not a girl in a love story.

Development

Students may need to use dictionaries to look up any unfamiliar words.

2 Choose one of the story types and write a story opening with your partner. Try to think of lots of words and descriptions that would suit the genre of your story.

Students should aim to write three paragraphs.

An alternative task:

- Sometimes it's good to subvert conventions. The first extract on the spread might not be suitable for a conventional love story, but it would make a great zombie romance!

  Some students might enjoy continuing this story themselves, imagining what might happen next, who the zombie girl is and what her lover might be like…

- Alternatively, ask students to take two of the genres in Development part 1 and produce a funny opening paragraph for a hybrid story, like a science fiction romance.

Chapter 8 AF8 Use correct spelling

1 Secure your basic spellings

Students will need access to dictionaries.

Development

It may help to photocopy the passage so students can annotate and correct it.

2 Spell -ly adverbs correctly

Students will need access to dictionaries.

Development

When students have finished, ask them to swap lists with a partner and test each other on ten adverbs. For each word you get one point if you get the correct -ly or -ily ending, plus another point if you spell the whole word correctly. At the end, write down your score out of 20.

Notes

Notes

Notes